California Government and Politics Today

Fifth Edition

Charles P. Sohner

Kentucky State University

Mona Field

Glendale Community College

SCOTT, FORESMAN/LITTLE, BROWN HIGHER EDUCATION
A Division of Scott, Foresman and Company
Glenview, Illinois   London, England

To Daniel S. Scott, with love and pride.
Charles P. Sohner

To my family, both those who dwell within my household and those beyond.
Mona Field

Library of Congress Cataloging-in-Publication Data

Sohner, Charles P.
    California government and politics today / Charles P. Sohner. Mona Field.—5th ed.
        p.   cm.
    Bibliography: p. 94
    Includes index.
    ISBN 0-673-39894-3
    1. California—Politics and government—1951–   I. Title.
JK8716.S63   1990
320.9794—dc20   89-10109
                                                                  CIP

Artwork, illustrations, and other materials supplied
by the publisher. Copyright © 1990 Scott, Foresman
and Company.

    2 3 4 5 6 —MAL—94 93 92 91 90

Preface

This new incarnation of a text first published more than 15 years ago attests to its continuing usefulness. If that interpretation, albeit self-serving, has some validity, we know it is because many suggestions of colleagues and students have been incorporated in its revisions. We remain in their debt as the fifth edition of *California Government and Politics Today* reflects more extensive changes than any of its predecessors.

These pages update the ever-changing panorama of California politics through the 1988 Fall elections. The chapters are reorganized somewhat, with a discussion of criminal justice after an examination of the court system. The concluding chapter is now devoted to a preview of the early 1990s. A glossary of important terms, italicized where they first appear in the text, will help students build their political vocabularies. The bibliography contains additional titles, a few of which place California government in the comparative context of its sister states. The appendix includes some organizational names and addresses to assist students interested in either research or enlistment as recruits.

Finally, this edition reflects the labor, erudition, and fresh perspectives of co-author, Mona Field. We join in urging readers to report their reactions to us and in thanking those prepublication reviewers who augmented our insights and corrected most of the errors for which we, still, must be held accountable. They include the following: Henry L. Janssen, San Diego State University; Donald R. Ranish, Antelope Valley College; John C. Syer, California State University, Sacramento; Don J. Wilson, Los Angeles City College. We are indebted also to the able and energetic Bruce Nichols, our editor at Scott, Foresman/Little, Brown. Members of our families, in various ways and at different times, provided forebearance, help, and inspiration. They did more than make the writing possible; they made doing it worthwhile.

Chuck Sohner
Mona Field

Contents

1

California Politics in Perspective

California is a model for the nation's future. Whether social, economic, or political, events in California consistently predate similar events in the United States as a whole. And most Californians, to the amusement and perhaps occasional resentment of others, identify as strongly with their state as with their country. Jo Anne Van Tilburg, an archaeologist, illustrates the point:

> During a stay on Easter Island, I was asked by one of the visitors where I was from. "California," I replied. He laughed and said, "Californians are the only people who respond to that question with the name of a state rather than a country."[1]

However chauvinistic, such pride of place is understandable. California, if it were a country, would rank sixth or seventh among the 170 or so nations of the world in Gross National Product.[2] Such an alluring and wealthy state has inevitable importance in national politics.

National Impact

California's remarkable influence on the nation probably began even before it became the thirty-first state on September 9, 1850. Presidential candidates have hailed from the Golden State since 1856, and, more recently, both Richard Nixon and Ronald Reagan helped bring a "Californocracy" to Washington by appointing substantial numbers of Californians to some of the federal government's most important posts.

Most of California's national influence flows from three traditional sources of political power—money, publicity, and population. Californians have more money than most Americans, with a statewide per capita income of $17,661—some $2,300 higher than that of the nation as a whole. The state's publicity edge stems chiefly from its preeminence in television and motion pictures. Huddled behind their snowed-in sidewalks and driveways, millions of Americans watch television on New Year's Day and wish they were in Pasadena, the City of Roses. Large numbers of these "wannabe-a-Californian" Americans do eventually visit or come to live in the state—many of them to find that the myth is larger than the reality.

It is sheer numbers, however, that contribute most substantially to California's political clout. With the nation's largest population, its residents outnumber those of second-place New York by a 3 to 2 margin (28 to 18 million). It has more than 10 percent of the seats in the House of Representatives and tops the nation with forty-seven *electoral votes*, the most coveted prize in a presidential election. Under such favorable circumstances, it is scarcely surprising that almost any prominent Californian might aspire to the presidency and other posts of national leadership.

The State and Its Citizens

Despite California's prominence in national affairs, the daily lives of its people are affected more closely by the politics of their own state. The state determines the grounds for divorce, the traffic regulations, the cost of public education, the penalties for drug possession, and the qualifications one needs to become a barber, psychologist, or lawyer. It establishes the amount of unemployment compensation, the location of highways, the subjects to be taught in school, and the rates to be charged by telephone, gas, and electric companies. Along with the local governments under its control, it regulates building construction, provides police and fire protection, and spends about 15 percent of the total value of goods and services produced by California residents.

The policy decisions made in these and other areas are influenced by the distribution of political power among various groups with competing needs and aspirations. Some of the power blocs reflect the same conflicts of interest that the nation experiences: labor vs. business; landlords vs. tenants; environmentalists vs. oil companies. But, as in so many things, these battles are fought on a grander scale in California. After Governor Deukmejian eliminated California's Occupational Safety and Health Administration on the grounds that it duplicated the federal OSHA, labor rapidly collected nearly 700,000 signatures (more than twice the number required) for a ballot *initiative* to restore Cal-OSHA and convinced the electorate to pass the initiative in November, 1988. The astronomical costs of housing have caused periodic election battles in cities such as Santa Monica and Berkeley over the issue of rent control. Because of the substantial amounts of oil off California's coast, and the equally vital importance of protecting the coastal environment, Californians frequently debate and vote on whether or not to develop these energy resources.

In addition to these battles, Californians struggle over how to absorb and assimilate their enormously diverse ethnic groups, how to best utilize scarce resources like water, and how to deal with vast differences in life-style and beliefs among the state's population. Ballot initiatives, often an indicator of which issues are closest to the hearts of the public, recently included such topics as how to cope with the AIDS crisis, the cost of automobile insurance, whether English should be the "official" language of the state, how much communities can continue to grow, and whether or not nuclear power plants should be closed. Whether the issue is approached through the legislative process or the initiative, the final outcome usually depends on such factors as money, political savvy, votes, and the elusive role of "big mo," the politicians' term for "momentum".

The State and the Nation

Like all states, California depends to a certain extent on the federal government to help support its programs. Much of the money arrives as *grants-in-aid* with many strings attached, while some is given more or less unconditionally as *block grants*. All told, the federal government supplies a substantial amount of revenue: In the 1983-84 fiscal year, California's counties got 22% of their total revenue from Washington, while its cities received nearly 8 percent.[3] Federal contracts to private corporations, many of them weapons manufacturers, channel still more money into the state, as do the paychecks to the 300,000 Californians employed directly by the national government.

Perhaps because of the heavy dependency of California's economy on federal defense contracts, Californians exhibit a peculiar voting pattern when it comes to issues of war and peace. In 1984, Los Angeles voters passed a local initiative calling for the city government to create a commission to study the fiscal impacts of converting from a military to a peace economy in the region. By 1986, aided by an expensive campaign from the defense industries that emphasized the immediate loss of jobs if the region were to de-militarize, the voters defeated a second initiative on the same topic. However, even as the voters manifest signs of confusion about these larger national issues, they can be grateful that the state's constitution permits direct voting on such topics. One wonders what the national political scene would be like if voters on a nationwide basis could vote on those matters that the federal government controls. Inasmuch as California so often leads the way for the nation, perhaps the day will come when "California-style" politics will spread, resulting in nationwide initiatives on vital matters confronting the entire country—matters foreshadowed by the issues and debates occurring in California today.

Reference Notes

1. Jo Anne Van Tilburg, "A State Apart", *Los Angeles Times Magazine*, Nov. 17, 1985, p. 43.
2. *Los Angeles Times*, April 5, 1987, Part IV, p. 2, and *Los Angeles Herald Examiner*, August 22, 1986, p. B-16.
3. *California Almanac*, 1986-1987, James S. Fay, senior editor (Novato, Calif. Presidio Press, 1985), pp. 10-9 and 10-16.

2

The Californians: Land, People, and Political Culture

The political process in California, as in other states, is conditioned by many geographic, demographic, and cultural influences. While geography changes very slowly, population shifts and cultural influences can inject new and unpredictable threads into the complex web that forms the state's identity and future prospects.

Geographic Influences

With an area of 156,000 square miles, California is larger than Italy, Japan, or England and trails only Alaska and Texas among the states. It is shaped like a gigantic stocking, with a length more than twice its width. If California were superimposed on the East coast, it would cover six states, from Florida to New York.[1] Those dimensions have contributed to an intense rivalry between the northern and southern portions of the state. Sectional controversy has occasionally prompted proposals that the state be divided in two and has been particularly sharp regarding the allocation of water supplies and funds for highway construction. The two sections differ enormously: the north is rainy, relies heavily on the lumber industry, and tends to be liberal; the south is dry, a major aerospace center, and a stronghold of conservative causes. The partisan differences are equally great. In the 1988 Congressional elections, Republicans won half the seats in the

House of Representatives from southern California districts but only 24 percent from northern and central California.

California's location has been at least as important as its size and shape. As the major state on what is called the Pacific Rim (those states bordering the Pacific Ocean and facing the Far East), it has attracted large numbers of Asians to its shores, led the nation in commercial fishing, and drawn huge federal investments in naval installations. Moreover, since the West was settled more recently than other parts of the nation, perhaps California has been more receptive to new ideas, such as the initiative and referendum, and the manager-council form of city government (to be discussed in Chapter 12.) The state is also one of only fifteen that borders a foreign nation. In part, as a result of the state's proximity to Mexico, Californians of Mexican descent have become the largest ethnic minority in the state, one which includes both first generation Americans and the "Chicanos" whose parents or ancestors originally came from Mexico. As an increasingly significant population group, California's Mexican Americans (and other Latinos as well) have been actively involved in extensive voter registration campaigns in order to convert their numbers into a potent political force.

Two other geographic influences command attention: rich natural resources and spectacularly alluring terrain. Between the majestic Sierra Nevada range along the eastern border and the Coastal Mountains on the west lies the Central Valley—one of the richest agricultural regions in the world. As a result, California leads the nation in farm output, even though, paradoxically, it ranks lowest among the states in percentage of population living in rural areas. Since over 40 percent of the state is forested, it ranks second in lumber production, while its petroleum resources place it third in oil supplies. Not surprisingly, agriculture, timber interests, and petroleum companies are major influences in state politics. The beauty and diversity of the natural landscape, ranging across arid deserts, a thousand-mile shoreline, and remote mountain wilderness, have made it a major battlefield in the war between conservationists and commercial recreation developers. About 45 percent of all land is federally owned (including five national parks and seventeen national forests), compared with less than 34 percent in the entire nation.

Despite the wondrous wealth conferred by California's geographic blessings, the chief rewards of that wealth are given only to a fortunate few. California leads the nation in millionaires, with more than 64,800, while 11 percent of its people live in poverty.[2]

Demographic Influences

There are at least two politically important characteristics of the California population. The first is the rapid growth that creates unprecedented demands for additional schools, freeways, and other government services. While the national population grew by 5.4 percent between 1980 and 1985, California's increased by 11.4 percent (see Table 2.1).

Growth, however, was uneven. Among major cities, San Francisco outpaced Los Angeles and San Diego. Even more impressive gains came in the agricultural heartland of the state, with cities such as Bakersfield, Stockton, and Fresno showing sizeable increases in population.

Along with the rest of the state, Southern California enjoyed an influx of large dimension. Los Angeles County grew more rapidly in the early 1980s than in the 1970s, and with five others in Southern California—Orange, Riverside, San Bernardino, San Diego, and Ventura—exceeded the combined population of the rest of the state. Growing at the fastest rate among these southern counties were Riverside and San Bernardino, combining to form what the Chamber of Commerce likes to call the "Inland Empire."

The second notable characteristic of the state's population is its diversity. California is becoming known as the "Ellis Island" of the 20th century as it forms the port of entry for immigrants from Asia and Latin America. In Orange County, the city of Westminster is known as "Little Saigon" due to the large numbers of Vietnamese who reside there. The city of Los Angeles, second largest in the nation, is now a *"minority—majority"* or *"Third World"* city. In fashionable Beverly Hills, one out of every six school children is Iranian, mostly political refugees who fled the tyranny of the Islamic revolution; Glendale, a bit to the northeast, has become the destination of large numbers of both Iranian and Soviet Armenians.

A good many ethnic concentrations have altered the identities of the communities in which they are located. They have left their marks in the languages of storefront signs, the foods sold in restaurants, the distinctive architecture of the buildings, and the preferences and prejudices reflected in neighborhood relationships and voting patterns.

The foreign-born immigrants who arrive in California reflect both a multitude of origins and multiple reasons for coming to the Golden State. In the late 1970s, Vietnamese flooded in after the defeat of

Table 2.1 Projected Population Change of California Counties
1980 to 2000
Ranked by Projected Percent Change

County	%Change	County	% Change
1. Alpine	100.0	31. San Bernardino	40.1
2. El Dorado	96.1	32. Sutter	40.0
3. Placer	74.4	33. Fresno	38.7
4. Solano	69.0	34. Monterey	38.2
5. Nevada	68.0	35. Yuba	37.1
6. Santa Cruz	67.3	36. Imperial	37.0
7. Mono	63.7	37. Merced	36.9
8. Tuolumne	60.2	38. San Joaquin	31.2
9. Mariposa	59.5	39. Glenn	30.9
10. Ventura	59.2	40. Sacramento	30.6
11. Lake	54.8	41. Lassen	30.2
12. Sonoma	52.0	42. Santa Clara	30.2
13. Madera	51.1	43. Tehama	29.8
14. Calaveras	50.5	44. Yolo	29.1
15. Napa	49.3	45. Kings	28.6
16. Butte	49.2	46. Contra Costa	28.0
17. Mendocino	49.0	47. Del Norte	26.8
18. Amador	48.2	48. Kern	26.1
19. Shasta	48.0	49. Santa Barbara	24.9
20. San Luis Obispo	47.7	50. Marin	22.7
21. Trinity	47.3	51. Colusa	21.1
22. San Diego	45.7	52. Modoc	20.2
23. Riverside	45.3	53. Siskiyou	18.9
24. Tulare	44.0	54. Humboldt	15.5
25. Pulmas	43.5	55. Los Angles	12.2
26. Stanislaus	42.7	56. Alameda	10.9
27. Sierra	42.4	57. San Mateo	10.3
28. Orange	42.1	58. San Francisco	-1.0
29. Inyo	40.3		
30. San Benito	40.2	The State	28.5

Source: California State Department of Finance, Population Research Unit

American allies in their country. In the 1980s, large numbers of Central Americans came to find refuge from the violence, poverty, and lack of opportunity in their homelands. Israelis, Russian Jews, Arabs, and Chinese immigrants are also among the many groups continually bringing new challenges to California.

Population diversity, however, involves more than ethnicity. "Sexual minorities" are now included in California's demographic vocabulary. While San Francisco is probably known as the heart of gay politics and community spirit, the relatively new city of West Hollywood (incorporated in 1985 by popular vote of the residents) had three homosexuals among its first five-member city council. After such political achievements as a state law to legalize all private sex acts by consenting adults (except for prostitution), the gay community now faces major challenges as it deals with its share of the AIDS crisis. This international epidemic has spawned several California ballot initiatives calling for a quarantine for all those who test positive for the AIDS virus. Thus far, the electorate has rejected all such drastic measures.

California's Political Culture

Each state has a distinctive political style that is influenced not only by geography, and population characteristics, but by the politically important attitudes and values shared by a substantial percentage of the people. These elements constitute what is sometimes called the *political culture*. In many ways, California's political culture is similar to that of the rest of the country. Californians are as devoted as any citizens to the principles of patriotism, capitalism, and democracy, no matter how nebulous such concepts may be. On the other hand, their frontier heritage perhaps includes a legacy of materialistic individualism, embodied in the modern "Yuppies," that may exceed that of other states.

From the State of the State messages given each year by California's governor, to the film industry's mythical depiction of fun in the sun, Californians and other Americans are bombarded with the images of impatient optimism and a sense of "special destiny" available in California. People come here expecting better things— gold in the mountains, oil in their backyards, or warm breezes rustling through the orange trees. With confidence based more on faith than on fact, they feel sure that there are jobs in the fields, aircraft factories, or movie studios. The many who find what they came for increase the frustrations of the many more who do not.

Their "grab the good life and damn the torpedoes" orientation makes gambling an important preoccupation for many Californians. Even before voters approved a state-operated lottery in 1984, California ranked second to Nevada in state tax revenue derived from various forms of gambling. When state lottery tickets went on sale at 21,000 locations in October of 1985, about 10 million $1.00 tickets were sold each day. Two months later, several supermarket chains reported that grocery sales had fallen by 5 percent, possibly because food money had been gambled on the lottery.

This constant quest for material success and the inevitable disappointment of those who don't "make good" may also help explain the appeal of extremist political movements offering panaceas for every problem. Although these movements have influenced California politics less than is sometimes supposed, they have been stronger here than in most other states. In the 1960s, on the far right of the political spectrum, the John Birch Society developed its major stronghold in Los Angeles and Orange Counties, while in Alameda County black leaders such as Bobby Seale and Huey Newton formed the Black Panthers as a leftwing political option for their communities. In recent years, California provided leadership for the right primarily through former Governor Ronald Reagan, both praised and reviled as the most conservative president in more than 50 years. Assemblyman Tom Hayden and actress Jane Fonda, have come to embody the left, especially as described by its critics, and Berkeley Representative Ron Dellums is one of the two members of Congress who are avowed Socialists through his membership in the Democratic Socialists of America.

Although these examples of non-centrist politics may be significant in the lives of some Californians, the average resident is far more seriously affected by social disruption and personal tragedy than by any variety of political extremism. Both suicide and alcohol-related deaths (chronic liver disease and cirrhosis), and the overall California crime rate, have exceed the national average by more than 20 percent. The divorce rate tops the country-wide norm by a fairly small margin, but the abortion rate exceeds the national average by more than 50 percent. These statistical indications of personal stress and desperation no doubt played a role in the 1986 legislation by Assemblyman John Vasconcellos (D-San Jose) who created a 25-member task force "to Promote Self-Esteem and Personal and Social Responsibility." This well-known assemblyman has long contended that the underlying causes of many social ills lie in the lack of both personal pride and communal responsibility in our society. He has made it his lifelong political struggle to encourage development of new forms of personal consciousness as well as new styles of interpersonal relationships for all Californians. This, too, reflects the uniqueness of the California political culture.

Reference Notes

1. *Los Angeles Times*, December 17, 1987, Part I, p. 3.
2. *California Almanac*, 1986–1987, James S. Fay, senior editor, (Novato, California: Presidio Press, 1985), p. 14–1.

3

California's Constitutional Development

The geographic, demographic, and cultural factors just described have had a major impact on the evolution of California government. In contrast, the historical background of the state has been altered so rapidly that it has left few permanent effects. The first period of development, when Indians were the only residents, has few traces today. With the arrival of the Europeans, however, records were maintained that provide some glimpses into later periods.

Spanish Beginnings

In 1542, only fifty years after Columbus "discovered the New World," Spain claimed California as a result of a voyage by Juan Rodriguez Cabrillo. Perhaps because California Indians were less economically advanced than those farther south in Mexico and Peru, Spain waited more than two centuries before establishing a permanent colony. The Spanish period truly began in 1769 with the settlement of San Diego by an expedition headed by Gaspar de Portola, a military commander, and Junipero Serra, one of the greatest missionaries of the Catholic Church.

Mexican Dominance

In 1822, Mexico gained control of California through the revolutionary overthrow of Spanish rule. Church influence was diminished, civilian governments were established for the pueblos, or villages, and Monterey was retained as the provincial capital. Yet California was still viewed as a remote colony, as much by the Mexicans as by the Spaniards. Within a few years, American explorers began to arrive, followed by a few settlers in the 1840s. The Americans were attracted by California's natural harbors and inviting climate and were inspired by their vision of a *"manifest destiny"* to control the whole continent. When the United States was rebuffed in its attempt to purchase California, it used a Texas boundary dispute as an excuse to launch the Mexican War in 1846. During the war, a few American military agents declared California an independent nation and named it the Bear Flag Republic. The Bear Flag rebellion was soon quashed, leaving California's current state flag as its only legacy. By 1847, California was brought under American military rule. After the defeat of Mexico in 1848, the Treaty of Guadalupe Hidalgo acknowledged U.S. possession of California and guaranteed legal rights and a bilingual system to the Mexican Californians.

Americanization

The U.S. military occupation lasted three years. Congress, which normally places newly acquired lands under territorial government, was immobilized by a dispute over whether to permit slavery in its newest possession. Before the issue could be settled, gold was discovered in 1848, making California land the most highly prized in the entire world. In 1849, the year of the legendary "gold rush," the settlers adopted their own constitution, largely pieced together from constitutional fragments adopted earlier by Iowa and New York. The California Constitution of 1849 activated a state government prohibiting slavery, but it had only provisional authority. Senator Henry Clay's *Compromise of 1850* temporarily settled the slavery dispute by mandating California's prohibition of slavery and admitting California as the thirty-first state. It was the first time a state that did not border an existing one entered the union. The transition to statehood would probably have taken longer had it not been for the discovery of gold and the influence of California's first United States senators, John C. Fremont, an explorer and military hero, and William Gwinn, a former southern politician and a dominant influence in the 1849 Constitutional Convention.

California's political past can be divided then into: (1) the Indian period (?-1769); (2) the Spanish period (1769-1822); (3) the Mexican period (1822-1846); (4) the period of American military rule (1846-

1849); and (5) the period of the first state constitution (1849-1879). Yet, except for the Spanish-Mexican heritage in architecture, place names, and food, and the predominantly American legacy of the English language and a three-branch government, today's California is largely a product of the last hundred years or so.

The Current California Constitution

In 1879 the first state constitution was replaced by a new one that has lasted to the present day. This document resulted more from social and economic changes than from fundamental flaws in the original constitution. Gold mining had declined in importance, and southern California had increased in influence, partially as a result of the citrus fruit industry. Most significantly, the completion of the transcontinental railroad in 1869 (with its western terminus in Sacramento), the growth of manufacturing, and the job competition provided by Chinese immigrants combined to produce pressures for political change. Led by Denis Kearney, a union-based Workingman's Party helped produce a new constitution. It was loaded with anti-Chinese provisions later declared invalid as a violation of the U.S. Constitution and was burdened with policy details involving such topics as wrestling and nut trees.

Repairing the Damage

By 1960, the detailed *statutory-type* provisions of the state constitution had required more than 350 amendments. It had grown to four times the size of the New York Constitution, ten times that of the U.S. Constitution, and was, according to the chief justice of the state Supreme Court, "almost everything a constitution ought not to be."[1] Failures to draft an entirely new constitution led to the creation of a Constitutional Revision Commission in 1963 to improve the old one. Its proposals have modernized the constitution and reduced its length by more than one third.

The Progressive Legacy

During the 110 or so years that the second constitution has been in effect, the changes that affected it most were those produced by the *progressive movement* led by former Governor Hiram Johnson in

California and President Theodore Roosevelt nationally. From about 1900 to 1920, Progressives led the way in trying to make government more efficient and democratic. They believed that there were two major obstacles that stood in the way of those goals—old and sometimes corrupt political party organizations and unimaginably rich businesses willing and able to spend whatever money was necessary to guarantee desired government favors.

The progressives had remarkable success. Political parties were weakened by imposing rigid legal controls on their internal organization, and prohibiting candidates for city, county, school, and judicial office from revealing their party affiliation on the ballot.

In the struggle against corporate power there was also notable progress. The excessive power of the Southern Pacific Railroad, which had helped fuel the public's zeal for rewriting the state's first constitution, was still embodied in its vast property holdings—it owned 11 million acres, or one-fifth of all privately owned land in the state. The enormity of the monopoly made it an obvious target for the Progressives' reformist efforts. Its major stockholders—Charles Crocker, Leland Stanford, Collis P. Huntington, and Mark Hopkins—were the "Big 4" who allegedly dominated state politics. According to their critics, they had bought "the best state legislature that money could buy." Perhaps the clearest symbol of their diminishing power was the 1910 campaign of Hiram Johnson, during which he refused to ride on trains or be linked in any way with the Southern Pacific Railroad.

Possibly the most enduringly important legacies left by the Progressives were the initiative and referendum, discussed in Chapter 7, that permit voters to pass laws themselves should the legislature be dominated by "vested interests," and the recall, which enables voters to remove an elected official from office.

Amendment Procedure

The California Constitution can be amended by a two-step procedure. First, amendments may be proposed by a two-thirds vote in both houses of the legislature or by an initiative petition signed by eight percent of the number of voters who cast ballots in the last election for governor. Second, the proposed amendment must appear as a proposition on the ballot and must be approved by a majority of voters.

Basic Constitutional Principles

Like the national government, the California political system is characterized by freedom, democracy, and a separation of powers. Certain differences, however, deserve attention. Although the separation of powers involves the traditional three branches—legislative, executive, and judicial—each is marked by distinctive state characteristics. The California legislature shares lawmaking authority with the people through the initiative process; the governor's power is diminished by the popular election of several other executive officials; lower-court judges are chosen by the voters for six-year terms, and others must be confirmed periodically by the electorate.

The state constitution protects the same freedoms guaranteed by the U.S. Constitution; additionally, it provides for such rights as those to possess property, and to fish on public lands. Article I, Section 2 of the California Constitution stipulates that "All political power is vested in the people," and this proclamation of democracy is reflected in the election (rather than appointment) of a large number of officials, as well as in governing practices such as the initiative, referendum, and recall.

The state government differs most from the national government in its centralization of power. Whereas the nation is characterized by a *federal* system, with both the national and state governments possessing some independent powers, the state is a *unitary* system with cities, counties, and other units of local government exercising only those powers the state chooses to give them. As a result, there is far more legal uniformity throughout each state than within the entire nation.

Reference Notes

1. Phil S. Gibson, in a 1955 speech at the University of Southern California.

4

Freedom and Equality: California's Delicate Balance

As in all regions in capitalist democracies, people in California must continually reassess choices regarding personal freedom and social equality. *Civil liberties,* such as the freedoms of speech, press, and association, may conflict with *civil rights.* For example, the freedom of association can conflict with antidiscriminatory civil rights laws. While many traditionally male-only clubs, such as the California Club of Los Angeles and the Olympic Club of San Francisco, have claimed that the freedom of association protects them from laws requiring the admission of women members, both state courts and the U.S. Supreme Court have ruled that cities may force large social clubs where business is transacted to obey antidiscrimination measures (*New York State Club Association* v. *City of New York* 86-1836).

Freedom of Religion

While Article I, Section 4 of the California Constitution states that "The free exercise and enjoyment of religious profession and worship, without discrimination or preference, shall forever be guaranteed by this state," only three lines later this freedom is limited by the statement: "but the liberty of conscience hereby secured shall not . . . excuse acts of licentiousness, or justify practices inconsistent with the peace or safety of this State." Under this authority, the State Supreme

Court has ruled that families who profess religious beliefs that preclude their children from receiving medical treatment (such as devout Christian Scientists or Jehovahs Witnesses) can be prosecuted for manslaughter if a child dies after being treated with prayer rather than medical care.[1]

In another court decision affecting the rights of religious minorities, the State Supreme Court ruled that the constitutional principle of separation of church and state prohibits prayers or invocations of a religious nature at the graduation ceremonies of public schools in the state. Typical prayers invoking the phrase "Almighty God" have been viewed as potentially offensive since California's school children include many whose belief systems do not include this monotheistic concept.[2]

Freedom of Speech and Press

Californians have long insisted upon communicating in a variety of ways. In 1983, there were a larger number of newspapers in California than anywhere else in the nation as well as the most cable TV subscribers and FM radio stations.[3]

While the major media outlets are rarely challenged on their rights to publish or sell their products, forms of communication concerned with sexual matters or extremist political views often stimulate controversy in the ongoing constitutional battles over free speech rights. In 1987, the city of Glendale (long-known as a highly conservative community) attempted to prevent the sale of sexually explicit periodicals by banning the use of sidewalk newspaper racks. Although the city's officials claim that their ordinance was carefully designed to be fully constitutional, it has been challenged in the courts by free speech advocates. Other efforts to curb what some consider to be inappropriate freedoms include the 1986 Los Angeles ordinance which prohibits massage parlors, adult bookstores, sexually oriented movie theaters, and clubs with nude dancers from doing business within 500 feet of a residential neighborhood.

Equality: Testing the Limits

Along with their controversial struggles to exercise various freedoms, Californians have also been forced to confront a long history of racial bigotry. Prejudicial attitudes and discriminatory behaviors are as old as the state itself. In the ten years following American conquest, the Indian population was violently reduced by more than half. When the United States defeated Mexico in 1848, California Mexicans were offered the ignominious choice of leaving their lands or renouncing their Mexican citizenship. Soon after, in the period of economic stagnation of the 1870s, the Chinese immigrants who helped build the transcontinental railroads during the 1860s became the targets of serious manifestations of racism, including lynchings and the "Chinese exclusion" provisions of the 1879 state constitution (which attempted to limit Chinese occupational choice and immigration into the state).

Segregation in the Schools

In 1988, after more than 20 years of expensive and divisive legal battles, U.S. District Judge A. Wallace Tashima ruled that the Los Angeles School Board must "settle its differences" over school segregation with the National Association for the Advancement of Colored People (NAACP). While intentional (or *de jure*) segregation in schools was declared unconstitutional in 1954 by the U.S. Supreme Court, Los Angeles, among other cities, had argued that its schools were segregated *de facto*, that is by circumstances of housing patterns rather than the school board's intention. Los Angeles and San Francisco schools show the highest levels of segregation of black students among the cities on the West Coast, but throughout the area even worse segregation occurs for Latino students. Remedies for segregation remain elusive, however, because the urban districts now have so few white students that it is virtually impossible to create ethnically balanced classrooms.[4]

Segregation in Housing and Employment

In 1959, the California legislature joined the civil rights struggles by passing the Unruh Act, requiring equal service in all business establishments, and a fair employment practices act aimed at job discrimination. In the 1960s, a long battle over discrimination by property-owners in the sale or rental of their property ended with a court ruling confirming the Rumford Fair Housing Act's prohibition of such bias. Nevertheless, racial prejudices continue to foster residential segregation in many California cities.

Minority Representation

The political effectiveness of California's minorities has been diminished by several factors. One is that whites still outnumber them. While influxes of immigrants have added to the numbers and diversity of ethnic minorities, the largest groups continue to be Latinos, with almost one-fourth the population, Blacks with 7.5 percent, and Asian and Pacific Islanders with 8 percent. Nonhispanic whites such as Armenians, Arabs, and others of Middle Eastern origin are not tallied separately but will continue to emerge as distinctive social and political forces.

Inadequate voter registration and lack of financial resources have been the main obstacles to minority participation in the political process. Also, for recently arrived members of the ethnic minority communities, language barriers and culture shock often prevent full participation in the electoral arena.

California blacks began to build a considerable political base in the 1970s with the elections of Wilson Riles as State Superintendent of Public Instruction, Mervyn Dymally as lieutenant governor, and Tom Bradley as mayor of Los Angeles. These gains were later consolidated by the record-breaking tenure of Willie Brown, a San Francisco attorney, as Speaker of the Assembly (1981-the present). But gains for Latinos did not accelerate until the 1980s. Although the state legislature includes only a handful of Latinos, many more have been elected to city councils and school boards throughout the state. Some of these local gains were based on *redistricting*. In 1986, for example, the U.S. Supreme Court found that Los Angeles had *gerrymandered* its council districts so as to fragment Latino voters. After the Court ordered the redrawing of council district boundaries, Gloria Molina (who had served previously in the state assembly) won a seat on the L.A. City Council and joined the only other Latino member, Richard Alatorre (who had also been a member of the state legislature). A similar legal action against Los Angeles County has been initiated and that county's five Supervisorial Districts may yet have to be redrawn to allow the large hispanic population a voice.

Asian-Americans have also made gains. March Fong Eu, the first Asian-American to hold statewide office, is now in her fourth term as secretary of state. While there are no Asian-Americans in the state legislature at present, Mike Woo has become highly visible as the first Asian to sit on the L.A. City Council and Lily Chen served one term as mayor of nearby Monterey Park. Additionally, two Asian-Americans, Norman Mineta and Robert Matsui, represent Congressional districts in Northern California.

Sexual Politics

Women, having less money than men and fewer contacts in high places, suffer from some of the same political disadvantages as the ethnic minorities. They too are generally underrepresented in public office. Highly visible exceptions include former Mayor Dianne Feinstein of San Francisco, Mayor Maureen O'Connor of San Diego, and State Senators Diane Watson of Los Angeles and Marian Bergeson of Newport Beach. Yet even the thirteen women in the state assembly (out of 80 total members) and the four women in the senate (out of 40) are scarcely a proportional representation for their sex.

The only avowedly gay member of a prominent governing body in California is San Francisco Supervisor Harry Britt, who succeeded Harvey Milk, a pioneer activist in the Gay rights movement, after the latter's assassination.

Reference Notes

1. *Los Angeles Times*, November 11, 1988, Part I, p. 1.
2. *Los Angeles Times*, October 23, 1987, Part I, p. 3.
3. *California Almanac*, James S. Fay, senior editor, 1986-1987 edition, Presidio Press, Novato, CA.
4. *Los Angeles Times*, June 21, 1988, Part I, p. 1.

5

Media Influences and Pressure Groups

The political attitudes of the people are basic to a consideration of democratic government. They are reflected most vividly in polling booths and spring from opinions formed by the influence of families, friends, churches, schools, life experiences, the mass media, and pressure groups. Perhaps the last two of these are most distinctive in their impact on state politics.

The Mass Media

Because state and local politics have not been viewed as important enough to command viewer interest, most of California's television stations provide little reporting from Sacramento or the various city halls around the state. Nevertheless, because the issues that state and local government affect (such as urban growth, education, pollution, public safety, homelessness, and health care) are becoming so controversial, newspaper coverage of California's internal politics seems to be improving and is indispensable to the informed citizen.

Partly due to the size and diversity of the state, no politician can ignore the role of the media in a campaign. Image-making is serious business in California—more than $45 million was spent in the 1984 election alone by candidates for the state senate and assembly. Most of that money was spent on simply advertising the candidates' names and faces. Additionally, Californians are known for having launched the political careers of two actors, former U.S.

Senator George Murphy and Ronald Reagan. California's press and broadcast media, like those elsewhere, tend to endorse Republican candidates although the McClatchy newspaper chain, which includes the *Sacramento, Fresno,* and *Modesto Bees,* is more independent and pro-Democratic. The *Los Angeles Times,* once known for promoting conservative views in its editorials and headlines, is now known as one of the most balanced information sources on the West coast. It employs about a dozen reporters in Sacramento concentrating on state politics and hundreds of correspondents around the globe.

Economic Interest Groups

Perhaps even more important than the mass media in shaping public opinion are organized *pressure groups.* These have been unusually influential in California politics and often aid individual candidates by providing them with publicity, financial contributions, and campaign workers.

Like most others, business pressure groups avoid affiliation with either party, although their basic conservatism usually benefits Republicans more than Democrats. The influence of various business groups is indicated, in part, by the size and wealth of their member companies. Most of the state's most profitable corporations, including oil companies, insurance giants, utilities, banks, and military contractors, are linked together in pressure groups such as the Merchants and Manufacturers Association, the Western Oil and Gas Association, and the Association of California Insurance Companies.[1] Other major players in the lobby game are the California Association of Realtors, the California Medical Association, the Trial Lawyers Association, and the State Water Contractors, which represent industry groups;[2] the California Teachers Association and unions in the California Labor Federation (such as the United Farm Workers) represent labor interests (see Table 5.1).

Other Interest Groups

In addition to the business, professional and labor groups that donate money to candidates through their Political Action Committees, and later urge elected officials to adopt their views, California's political process also has enabled other interest groups to develop and

Table 5.1 *Major business organizations in California*

Associated Builders and Contractors of California, Inc.
Association of California Insurance Companies
California Apartment Association
California of Association of Realtors
California of Association of Thrift and Loan Companies
California Association of Tobacco and Candy Distributors
California Beer Wholesalers Association, Inc.
California Business Alliance
California Chamber of Commerce
California Hotel and Motel Association
California Independent Oil Marketers Association
California Manufacturers
California Railroad Association
California Restaurant Association
California Retail Liquor Dealer Association
California Trucking Association
Construction Industry Legislative Council
Independent Automobile Dealers Association of California
Insurance Agents and Brokers Legislative Council
Motorcycle Industry Council

Source: California Secretary of State, 1985-86 Lobbyist and Employer Registration Directory.

participate. Such groups include those representing various ethnic communities, environmental organizations such as the Sierra Club, the National Organization for Women, and single issue groups such as the Gun Owners of California and the Hell's Angels (whose lobby efforts deal almost exclusively with fighting legislation to require helmets for motorcyclists).

Government also lobbies itself as evidenced by the active involvement in Sacramento of lobbyists for various cities, counties, and school districts, and even the Metropolitan Water District of Southern California, which led the list of spenders in 1987 by reporting $1.86 million in lobbying expenses.[3]

Lobbyists in Action

The term *lobbying* began when those who wanted to influence elected officials would congregate in the lobbies of public buildings and wait to speak with politicians about their concerns. California's lobbyists, like those around the nation, gradually developed a pattern of wining and dining the politicians as well as giving them gifts and campaign contributions. Periodically, the public has demanded a clean-up of lobbying practices and a reduction in the power and influence of the interest groups. The 1974 Political Reform Initiative, which voters adopted by a two-thirds margin, requires each lobbyist to file monthly reports showing income, expenditures, and steps taken to influence government action. Although it had strict $10 per month limits on the value of meals, drinks, or other gifts a lobbyist could give a public official, its provisions were apparently insufficient for the public. In 1988, to the consternation of almost all politicians, voters approved two additional campaign reform initiatives, Propositions 68 and 73, both of which were advertised as methods to reduce the influence of special interests on legislators. Because both dealt with the same subject and were approved, the one with the most votes (Proposition 73) took effect and caused chaos in Sacramento as politicians scurried to figure out how the new law would affect their accumulated "war chests" and their future campaigns.

Some of the provisions of Proposition 73 prohibit transfers of campaign funds among candidates, limit donations collected in nonelection years, and bar use of public funds for campaigns. Supporters of the rival Proposition 68 remain critical of the fact that Proposition 73 does not limit campaign expenditures, and it is conceivable that a proposition designed to create expenditure limits may yet emerge for the voters' consideration. In any case, the ultimate interpretation of the new law will no doubt be determined in the courts as the lobbyists and elected officials struggle over the exact implications of the initiative. Meanwhile, the tactics of lobbyists remain the same, even as the rules for disbursing their financial largesse are adjusted. Highly paid, and generally trained as lawyers, major lobbyists utilize many of the following strategies:

1. campaign contributions to sympathetic candidates, especially incumbents;
2. testimony for or against bills being considered by legislative committees;
3. informal contacts with lawmakers for purposes of providing them with information, statistical data, and expert opinions on pending legislation;
4. newspaper and other advertising designed to influence public officials indirectly by molding public opinion;
5. sponsorship of initiative petitions to put propositions on the ballot for the approval of the voters;
6. encouragement of pressure group members to write letters to lawmakers regarding particular bills;

7. organization of protest marches and other forms of public demonstrations;
8. attempts to influence the appointment of sympathetic judges and administrative officials.

Members of the public who wish to trace the impact of lobbying on their elected officials should compare donations to their legislators with the voting records. This may indicate the role of a particular pressure group in influencing a politician's vote. Because lobbying efforts fluctuate depending on which issues are "hot," voters must watch for overall patterns in campaign contributions and subsequent votes by legislators. Valuable sources of information include the Consumers' Union reports on campaign contributions, which divulge data such as 1987 figures revealing that the insurance industry and the trial lawyers were the top two political contributors in the state. This was the year that the legislature could not get an insurance reform act passed and in which five insurance initiatives sprouted for the November, 1988 ballot.[4] (Interestingly enough, despite the $76 million that the insurance industry and trial lawyers spent to promote their competing initiatives, the only insurance initiative that won was the Consumer Revolt Initiative sponsored by Ralph Nader.) The Fair Political Practices Commission also prepares annual reports on campaign donations, and various interest groups compile lists of so-called "right" or "wrong" votes cast by the lawmakers.

Reference Notes

1. *Los Angeles Times*, April 24, 1988, Business Part II, p. 8, "Is Bigger Better?" by Douglas Frantz.
2. *Los Angeles Times*, April 13, 1988, p. 3, "$75 Million Spent in 87 by Lobbies, FPPC Says."
3. Ibid.
4. *Los Angeles Times*, May 17, 1988, "Insurance Firms' Gift to Governor, Legislators Told," by Kenneth Reich, p. 3.

6

Political Parties and Other Voluntary Associations

The two major parties seem to be of even less importance to the average Californian than to most Americans. Often they neither command respect nor determine ballot choices for major offices. Many citizen activists remain almost entirely separate from party organizations yet are immersed in the *grassroots* political process through an enormous variety of voluntary associations. Some, like many Parent-Teacher Associations and homeowner groups, have become highly politicized. Activities that used to require volunteers with time and energy and little political awareness now require participants who understand the intimate links between one's neighborhood problems or local school issues and the larger California political process.Parents of children in overcrowded schools, homeowners concerned about graffiti, and beach lovers whose beaches are polluted are among many Californians whose political involvement begins when they collect signatures for ballot initiatives or lobby public officials in an effort to resolve their particular problems.

Meanwhile, despite the scarcity of Californians who participate directly in their political parties or feel any special enthusiasm for either party, party affiliations are reflected in the voting patterns of legislators and the track records of governors. On many issues of major public concern, such as abortion, criminal justice, and funding for education, the majority party in the legislature can heavily influence the final outcome—and the votes of individual legislators may depend more on party allegiance than on any other factor.

The Weakness of Parties in California

Though neither party is as weak as it once was, several factors in California have served to reduce the influence of both. The *civil service system* fills 98 percent of all state government jobs on the basis of competitive exams, thereby reducing the number that can be used as *patronage* to reward supporters of the winning party. Local offices (including city, county, and school boards) and judicial elections are *nonpartisan*, with ballots omitting the party affiliation of the candidates. The ballot format itself, known as the *office-block ballot*, groups candidates under the heading of the office being contested, and thus encourages voters to concentrate on individual candidates rather than voting a straight party ticket. Finally, state laws regulating the parties' organizational structures tend to reduce their effectiveness.

In addition to these many obstacles to "party power," during certain eras the political differences between the two major parties have blurred to the point that neither presented a distinctive choice for voters.During these times, third parties have sometimes gained a small foothold in the political process. However, during all of the 1980s, Democrats and Republicans in the legislature have provided a fascinating spectacle of intense partisanship as evidenced by the *California Journal's* 1988 study of voting records showing that more than 80 percent of legislators almost never vote against their party's leadership.[1] In the executive branch, the Deukmejian era reinforced Sacramento's *partisan* divisions as the Governor quickly emphasized that he would insist on a conservative approach to budget matters, expect strong support from the legislature's Republican leaders, and respond to the Democrats' pressures with an iron fist and a sharp blue pencil (the symbol of his veto powers). Although the "Iron Duke" won many of his battles with the Democratic legislators, one of his worst defeats was the 1988 rejection of his nominee for state treasurer, Congressman Daniel E. Lungren—a defeat that Deukmejian openly blamed on the Senate's Democrats.

Perhaps this type of highly publicized partisan battle will re-awaken the electorate's interest in political parties, but working against this possibility is the ever-more-prominent role of media and money in campaigns—a role that discourages party and issue-oriented politics and encourages image-based voting both on candidates and ballot propositions.

Third Parties

Although the Workingman's Party, leading the attack against both Chinese workers and exploitive corporations, had a major impact on the constitution of 1879, third parties have had relatively little influence on politics within the state since that time. Both major parties, in fact, have made it difficult for them to get on the ballot. In the late 1960s, motivated by dissatisfaction with the Republicans and Democrats, activists from both the left and right attempted to register the 1 percent of voters needed to get new parties on the California ballot. Many did not succeed in getting on the statewide ballot but did raise issues and put pressure on mainstream politicians. On the left, La Raza Unida party focused on the farmworkers' struggle to unionize, while the Peace and Freedom Party appealed to those opposed to U.S. involvement in Vietnam. On the right, the American Independent Party tapped conservatives dissatisfied with election choices, and was soon followed by the Libertarian Party which advocated *minimalist* government. Of these, only candidates of the La Raza Unida Party are no longer on the ballot.

Party Organization

For those who choose party activism as a route to political involvement, one path leads to membership in county committees or state central committees (see Figure 6.1). State central committees include one to two thousand people and include elected officials and candidates, as well as the county committee chairpersons. The size of *county committees* varies depending on the county's population. Their members are elected in the *primaries* by voters who often select randomly from a list of unfamiliar names. Almost any interested person can get involved at the County Committee level—in some cases there are barely enough candidates to fill the number of positions available. Some of the more important functions of the state committee are to draft the state party platform and to assist campaigns for party nominees. County committees contribute by raising funds and registering voters.

Virtually the only time controversy occurs in these elections is when extremist groups such as Lyndon LaRouche's quasi-fascist organization have their members run for county committee posts in one of the two major parties. The LaRouchites' goal is to "infiltrate"

Figure 6.1 Organization structure—Republican State Central Committee

STATE CONVENTION

Republican Nominees
National Committeeman
National Committeewoman
Chairman and Vice Chairman
of the State Central Committee
Selected County Committee Chairmen

EXECUTIVE COMMITTEE

State Committee Officers
National Committeeman and
Committeewoman
Republican U.S. Senators
Representatives of California
Republican Congressional, State,
and Assembly Delegations
Presidents of State-wide Volunteer
Organizations
Selected County Committee Chairmen
Officers of Association of Republican
County Central Committee Chairmen
Appointed Members

STATE CENTRAL COMMITTEE

Convention Delegates
Appointed Members
County Central Committee Chairmen
Past Chairman of the State Central
Committee

STATE CHAIRMAN

BOARD OF DIRECTORS

ADMINISTRATION

Platform
Proxies & Credentials
Resolutions
Rules

COMMUNICATION
AND RESEARCH

Publications
Press

SPECIAL PROJECTS

Youth Committee
Nationalities
County Central
Committee Liaison
Speakers Bureau
New Ways
Special Committees

FINANCE

FIELD
DIRECTOR

CAL PLAN

PRECINCT COMMITTEE

FIELD STAFF

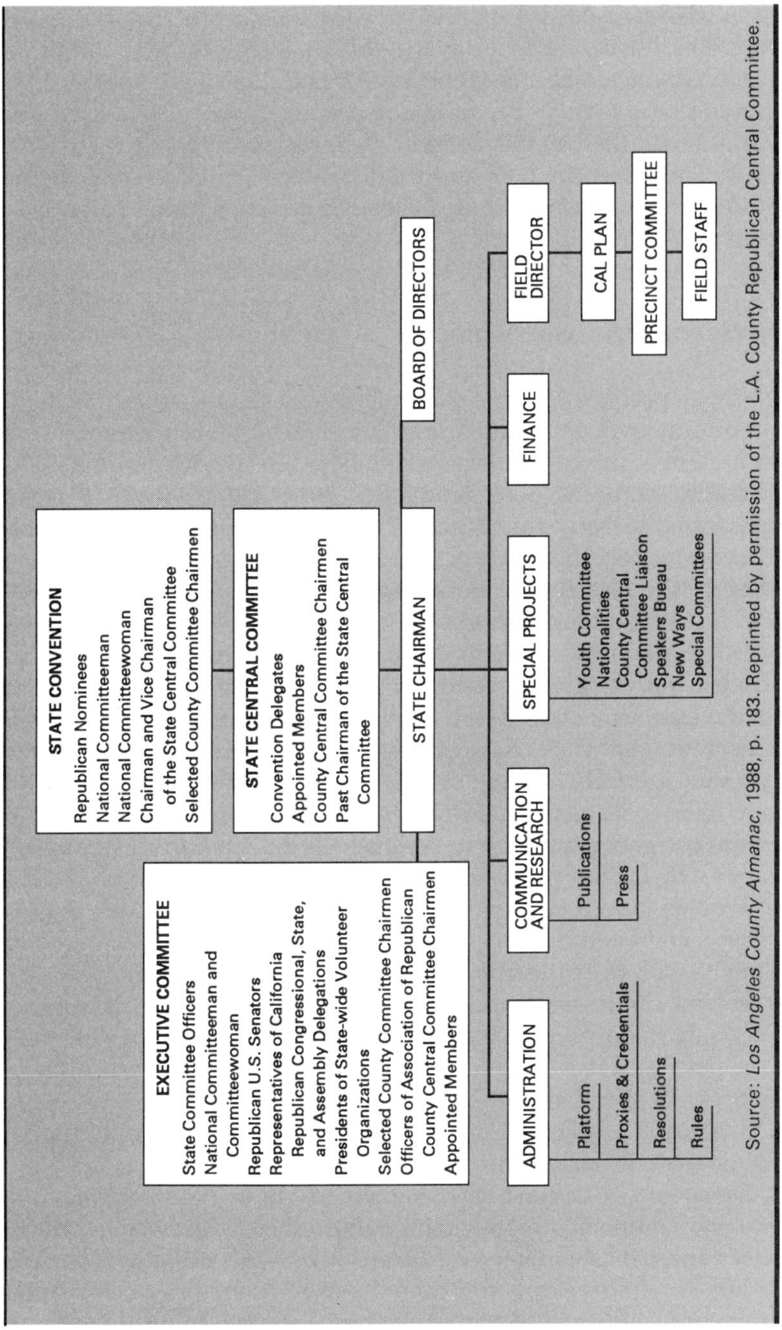

Source: *Los Angeles County Almanac*, 1988, p. 183. Reprinted by permission of the L.A. County Republican Central Committee.

the mainstream parties, particularly the Democrats, by running for committee posts and even as candidates for office, a situation that causes extreme embarrassment when a LaRouchite wins due to voter ignorance. (A similar predicament occured when a Ku Klux Klan member won the Democratic party's nomination for a congressional seat in San Diego in 1985 and the local Democratic leaders ruefully withdrew their support from their own nominee rather than help a political extremist into office).

Partisan Volunteer Groups

The legal party structure just described lacks organization at the community level and therefore is unable to establish neighborhood headquarters or enlist necessary campaign workers. It also has difficulties recruiting good candidates, especially for the state senate and assembly. To compensate for these deficiencies, party loyalists have banded together to form statewide volunteer organizations. The oldest of these is the California Republican Assembly, founded in 1934. It fostered the creation of local Republican clubs and endorsed and supported candidates in the months preceding the primary. The CRA enjoyed so much success in revitalizing the Republican party that the Democrats followed its example in establishing the California Democratic Council (CDC) in 1953. Over the years, factional disputes disrupted the CRA, giving rise to a more conservative group, the United Republicans of California. Moderates in the party, unwelcome in either organization, then established the California Republican League—by far the weakest of the three. The Federation of Republican Women stayed largely outside the battle and, as a result, has the largest membership of any GOP group in the state. Rigid right-wing elements took over the Young Republicans, a club of some influence on several campuses throughout the state. Republican Associates, which makes no preprimary endorsements, works with all elements of the party and has its base of support among business executives; it has been an effective fund-raiser and conducts training sessions for GOP precinct workers. Lincoln clubs also raise money to support Republican candidates and committees.

Democrats, too, have been subject to divisive ideological battles that have diminished membership within their CDC. Many younger liberals and radicals prefer to affiliate with organizations that are even less linked to party structures than the CDC itself. One such group is Campaign California, composed primarily of middle-aged and younger people whose political roots lie in the civil rights, antiwar, and women's movements of the 1960s. Headed by Assemblyman Tom Hayden (D-Santa Monica), the organization was originally known as the Campaign for Economic Democracy and was famous for funneling the profits of Jane Fonda's Workout programs to candidates throughout the state who advocated rent control and environmental protection. In the 1970s some of these candidates became city council members in cities such as Berkeley, Chico, and Santa Monica, and Hayden himself was propelled into the State Assembly in 1982 after waging the most costly campaign in California legislative history. In 1986 Campaign California took much of the credit for the passage of Proposition 65, the Safe Drinking Water, and Toxic Enforcement Act.

Nonpartisan Political Associations

Outside the party structure and party-oriented organizations are the multitude of *grassroots* groupings which, for many people, *are* California politics. Perhaps the growing popularity of such groups reflects the historical weakness of parties and the current low profiles of the partisan organizations. Or perhaps the issues that confront Californians daily are best approached through *issue-oriented organizations* with no absolute loyalty to any party. In many respects, such organizations are a variety of the pressure groups discussed in the last chapter. Most of the ones discussed below, however, rely more on involvement by average citizens and somewhat less on monetary influence or professional lobbying expertise. They are usually concerned, moreover, with influencing government policy primarily at the local, and sometimes even the neighborhood, level.

For those concerned with environmental protection, groups such as Save our Coast (based in San Mateo), Heal the Bay (Los Angeles), the League of Conservation Voters (statewide), and the People for Open Space/Greenbelt Congress (San Francisco area) are in constant need of volunteers' time, energy, and money. For women seeking greater representation, the California chapters of the National Women's Political Caucus, the Hollywood Women's Political Committee (composed of high-power, affluent women from the entertainment industry), the Coalition of Labor Union Women, and the Los Angeles-based Fund for A Feminist Majority all raise money and organize volunteers to get women into office as well as to elect men sympathetic to women's concerns.

Activist blacks and latinos are involved in California affiliates of the Southern Christian Leadership Conference, the National Association for the Advancement of Colored People, the Mexican American Political Association, the United Neighborhood Organization, and the Mexican American Legal Defense and Education Fund, all of which encourage minority involvement in both electoral politics and community issues. Asian Americans, the second fastest growing minority group (Latinos are the first), derive much of their political clout from the Asian Pacific American Legal Center of Southern California. All of these groups concern themselves with the ongoing issues of minorities, including school integration, bilingual education, affirmative action, and employment and housing opportunities.

Among the newer and more vigorous forms of voluntary association in California are the *slow-growth* or controlled-growth movements. From tiny Tiburon in the north to sprawling Los Angeles in the south, groups are coalescing both at the neighborhood level and in regional networks to respond to the complex issues raised by the constant population growth of the state. A study done by the Center for Continuing Study of the California Economy predicts a 17 percent population increase (from 28 million to 32 million) by 1995, and the difficulties of providing jobs, housing, education, and recreation for all Californians will escalate in proportion to those numbers.[2] Working alongside the slow-growth groups are the historic preservationists who battle continually to protect architectural and cultural landmarks from demolition.

Add to this melange the education-oriented groups such as the Parent-Teacher Association and Parent Advisory Councils, the political reform groups such as Common Cause, and the hundreds of other civic-minded associations throughout the state, and California's opportunities for voluntary political activism become readily apparent.

Reference Notes

1. *California Journal*, June 1988, p. 243.
2. *Los Angeles Times*, January 27, 1988, Part IV, p. 2

7

Campaigns and Elections

California has a *closed primary* within each party, meaning that only voters who indicate a preference for a particular party when they register to vote may vote in that party's primary election. The primary is held the first Tuesday after the first Monday in June to nominate candidates for state and national office. If a voter declines to state a party choice or names a party not qualified for the ballot, he or she will receive a short ballot listing only the names of candidates running for nonpartisan posts and the propositions submitted for a yes-or-no vote.

A registered voter may run for an office in the primary by filing a declaration of candidacy with the county clerk at least sixty-nine days before the election, paying a filing fee (unless he swears that he cannot afford it), and submitting a petition with the signatures of from 20 to 500 registered voters, depending on the office sought. In a partisan primary race, the party nomination is won by the candidate with the largest number, or *plurality,* of votes. In a nonpartisan contest, however, if no candidate receives a *majority* (50 percent plus one), the two with the most votes face one another in a later *runoff election.* Nonpartisan elections are held for city, county, judicial, and school board offices.

The Road to Victory

It is easy to run for office in California, but to win requires a combination of campaign ingredients difficult to assemble. One of the most important is an "electable" candidate. Because of the many voters who are recent arrivals in the state and the frequency with which they move, a candidate's longstanding community ties and a wide personal acquaintance are not as important here as elsewhere in the nation. Name recognition is important, however, and gives a decided advantage to one (such as Ronald Reagan) who has established a wide reputation in another field or has a famous family name (such as former Governor Jerry Brown whose father was a governor before him). Even a family name that is familiar due to completely nonpolitical reasons may help a politician get started. John Van de Kamp of the Van de Kamp's restaurant and bakery family is Attorney General of California.

Money and Politics

Campaigns are now so expensive that one of the greatest dangers to democratic politics is that races will be won by the biggest spenders rather than the best candidates. This problem is well-illustrated by the differences in financial support between incumbents (whose status as officeholders provides name identification and easy access to donations) and any newcomers to the political scene. In the 1986 state legislative races, assembly incumbents outspent challengers by 30-to-1 while senate officeholders had a 62-to-1 financial edge over their opponents.[1] Not a single incumbent was turned out of office, although opinion surveys indicated that public confidence in lawmakers was extremely low.[2] The public can only speculate on what the various challengers might have been able to achieve in politics since their efforts to take office were uniformly unsuccessful.

Despite pollster Mervin Field's conclusion that TV ads are "not too efficient" as a way to reach voters because so many of the political commercials reach nonvoters, politicians spend enough money on campaigns and particularly on TV ads, to cover the costs of some of the most needed services in the state. In 1984, legislative candidates alone spent almost $45 million, while in 1986, the gubernatorial race between incumbent Deukmejian and challenger Tom Bradley cost more than $20 million. Add to this the $130 million spent in 1988 on efforts to pass or defeat the various ballot propositions, and, over a four-year period, well over $200 million was spent on state elections. This is precisely the amount that officials in San Diego and Imperial Counties were pleading for in 1985 in order to clean up the dangerous contamination in the Tijuana River.[3]

With relatively few Californians voting, it would seem that those who aspire to elective office would spend their campaign dollars on direct mail communications with those voters who show a regular pattern of going to the polls. In fact, local city and school board elections often depend on this kind of targeted mailing. But state legislative and county supervisorial candidates frequently spend large amounts on TV ads, much of which is wasted on nonvoting television viewers and on people living outside the district.

The millions of campaign dollars come from a variety of sources. The Fair Political Practices Commission, set up by voters in 1974, estimates that nearly half of all funds are donated by business interests; about 10 percent by agricultural groups; 8 percent by labor unions and public employee associations; and almost 11 percent by individual contributors. The remaining 20 percent or so is provided by political parties.[4]

Although few Californians meet their candidates in person, those who are registered to vote may find themselves answering the doorbell during election season to find a dedicated campaign volunteer. Door-to-door personal efforts are most effective in local races, where even a less well-funded newcomer can defeat an incumbent when the electorate's mood is right. Los Angeles City Councilwomen Pat Russell and Peggy Stevenson, both with years of experience and good financial resources, were defeated by challengers due to this kind of campaign organization as well as a large reservoir of voter frustration with their policies.

A final outlet for California campaign expenditures is the use of public relations firms to run campaigns. In return for large fees, "PR" experts devise slogans, film TV commercials, write advertising copy, design billboards, and aid in the general development and implementation of campaign strategy.

Campaign Reform

Due to accumulated pressures from both public interest groups such as Common Cause, and the Fair Political Practices Commission itself, a number of ballot initiatives emerged in the late 1980s that offered potential relief from the enormous influence of money in elections. As with many political issues, it took several years before voters felt sufficiently disgruntled to vote for a new law—even voters who have some understanding of a political problem may mistrust the various solutions presented to them at the ballot box and vote them down.

When the voters finally acted in 1988, however, they passed two different campaign reform initiatives in the same election, Propositions 68 and 73. For the first time, limits were placed on donations to state and local campaigns. Although the full impact of the propositions is still being decided in the courts, basic provisions limit donations to a candidate to $1000 from an individual or $5000 from a *Political Action Committee* (PAC). PACs are usually created by corporations, unions, or some other pressure group to solicit donations, which are then contributed to candidates endorsed by the group; even with the new limits, PACs may find loopholes by "subdividing" into more PACs, each of which can give up to $5000.

Both initiatives also prohibit transfers of contributions from one candidate to another, thus diminishing the powers of such successful fundraisers as Willie Brown, longtime Speaker of the Assembly, who raised and then gave away to fellow Democrats over $1 million for the 1984 legislative races.

Even prior to Proposition 73's passage, the Fair Political Practices Act of 1974 required that any donation of $100 or more must be reported to the FPPC so that the public may know which politicians receive money from which sources. Traditionally, Republican candidates show stronger support from corporate and small business interests, while Democrats receive more donations from labor groups. But politics makes strange bedfellows, and almost all politicians take funds from whoever is willing to give.

The changes brought about by Propositions 68 and 73 may represent only the beginning of reform. As mentioned in Chapter 5, continued efforts to allow public financing of campaigns in California may arise as voters realize that private interests and the incumbents who get most of their support, still dominate the process.

The Voter Decides

California women gained the right to vote in 1911, eight years before the U.S. Constitution extended that right across the nation. Today, however, most state voting requirements have been superseded by federal regulations, and virtually all citizens eighteen years of age or older are eligible to cast their ballots if they have registered in advance.

Though the majority of Californians are eligible to vote, the likelihood that they will exercise this right varies substantially from group to group. For the most part, voter turnout is highest in districts with well-educated, well-to-do, overwhelmingly white populations. The patterns of voter registration by race and class have been so obvious that in 1986 the Superior Court of Los Angeles County ruled that county health and social service workers may register voters on the grounds that the government should promote voter registration among low-income and minority citizens.

Once they arrive at the polls, Californians have an almost schizophrenic approach to election choices. For executive branch races, despite registration figures that indicate that about 50 percent of California voters are Democrats and 40 percent are Republicans (the remaining voters are either members of the minor parties or independents), many people cross party lines to vote for the individual candidate of their choice. Thus, in the November 1986 election, 37 percent of the Democrats voted for Republican George Deukmejian for governor, while 24 percent of the Republicans voted for Democrat Leo McCarthy in the lieutenant governor's race.[5] For congressional offices and the state legislature, on the other hand, voters tend to stick to their party's candidates. For this reason, voter registration has become increasingly important to both parties as they seek to increase their vote totals.

Direct Democracy

Across the nation, the phrase "voter apathy" has become a regular topic of discussion during each election season. Opinion polls repeatedly indicate that voters view politics as "dirty, crooked, and corrupting"[6] and thus prefer to ignore the political process. At the same time, many citizens feel powerless in the face of the large amounts of money used in political campaigns. While such feelings of distaste and powerlessness are understandable, these concerns ought not be the pretext for millions of Americans to abandon their political responsibilities. More so than in most states, California voters have constitutionally insured mechanisms to influence public policy such as the direct democracy devices that permit the voters to bypass elected officials and make policy themselves.

The use of direct democracy by American state governments dates back to the Progressive reform movements of the early 1900s. In contrast to the federal government, in which elected or appointed representatives make all the decisions for the public, California's constitution assures that the state's voters can make laws, repeal laws, or recall their elected officials through the ballot box.

The *initiative* process permits registered voters to place a proposed law on the ballot through petition signatures equal to 5 percent of the votes cast in the last election for governor. Amendments to the state constitution require 8 percent. In either case, if the proponents of the initiative succeed in gathering enough valid signatures in the 150 days permitted, the measure appears on the ballot as a numbered proposition and is approved by a simple majority vote. Although the initiative was designed to counterbalance the power of lobbyists on the legislature, pressure groups now employ it to gain approval of measures that the state legislature rejects. Sometimes pressure groups hire professional petition circulators to obtain the necessary signatures and then advertise heavily to win voter approval. Since the initiative's first use in 1912, slightly more than 200 measures have qualified for the ballot (out of approximately 660 circulated) and about 60 of these have actually become laws.

There are two kinds of *referendums*, one of which embodies the same spirit as the initiative. This so-called "protest" referendum allows 5 percent of the voters to sign a petition placing on the ballot a law already passed by the legislature. A simple majority vote can repeal the legislature's original action. Due to the requirement that all signatures must be gathered within 90 days of the legislation's passage, the use of this type of referendum has generally been quite rare. Since 1911, protest referendums have reached the ballot only 39 times, with 25 of these passing.

The second type of referendum is one submitted to the voters by the legislature rather than by petition. The state constitution requires that all legislative efforts to borrow money by the sale of bonds as well as all constitutional amendments proposed by the legislature be approved by the voters. Also, if the legislature wishes to amend a law passed by initiative, such amendments must also be placed on the ballot for consideration by the voters.

The third component of what is generally referred to as "direct democracy" is the *recall*. It is a device by which voters can petition for a special election to remove an official from office before his or her term has expired. Although two state senators have been unseated by recall elections and several governors have been targets of recall petitions, recalls have generally been restricted to city, county, and school officials. A recall petition normally requires the signatures of 12–25 percent of the voters; if that requirement is met, opposing candidates may file for places on the ballot. Voters must then vote on whether or not to recall the official and which of the other candidates to elect to fill the possible vacancy. Because voter hostility toward an

Table 7.1 *November 1988 ballot propositions*

Proposition 78–Higher Education Bond **Passed**
Proposition 79–School Bond **Passed**
Proposition 80–Prison Construction Bond **Passed**
Proposition 81–Safe Drinking Water Bond Law **Passed**
Proposition 82–Water Conservation Bond Law **Passed**
Proposition 83–Clean Water Bond Law **Passed**
Proposition 84–Housing and Homeless Bond **Passed**
Proposition 85–Library Construction Bond **Passed**
Proposition 86–County Jail Construction Bond **Passed**
Proposition 87–Property Taxation **Passed**
Proposition 88–Deposit of Public Money **Passed**
Proposition 89–Governor's Parole Review **Passed**
Proposition 90–Assessed Property Value **Passed**
Proposition 91–Justice Courts **Passed**
Proposition 92–Judicial Performance **Passed**
Proposition 93–Veterans' Tax Exemption **Passed**
Proposition 94–Judges **Passed**
Proposition 95–Homeless Funds **Defeated**
Proposition 96–AIDS Tests **Passed**
Proposition 97–Cal OSHA **Passed**
Proposition 98–School Funding **Passed**
Proposition 99–Cigarette Tax **Passed**
Proposition 100–Auto Insurance Rates **Defeated**
Proposition 101–Auto Insurance Claims **Defeated**
Proposition 102–AIDS Reporting **Defeated**
Proposition 103–Insurance Rates & Regulations **Passed**
Proposition 104–No-Fault Insurance **Defeated**
Proposition 105–Public Disclosures **Passed**
Proposition 106–Attorney Fees **Defeated**

Source: California Secretary of State's Office, Elections Division.

official must be immense for a recall to be successful, it has now mostly become a means to put pressure on an unpopular or ineffective incumbent. Often the pressures created by the circulation of a recall petition can force a politician to change some policies or even to resign. Both former Chief Justice Rose Bird and Los Angeles City Councilman Art Snyder were severely pressured by recall efforts in the 1980s, but neither left office due to recall. (Bird was forced out of office in a confirmation election vote and Snyder eventually resigned to become a lobbyist.)

The Progressives intended for the initiative, referendum, and recall to be methods by which citizens could make policy directly or remove incompetent officials, thus counteracting the corruption of a state legislature that might prostitute itself to rich and powerful special interests. Instead, those same special interests have sometimes used these techniques to seduce the voters into giving them privileges that the politicians would not. Since about 370,000 signatures are necessary for the voters to place a statutory initiative on the ballot (and almost 600,000 required for a constitutional amendment), many contend that this is a technique available only to powerful pressure groups. Other critics argue that proposition measures are too complex for average citizens to understand and too long for them to read. These criticisms are especially valid when voters have a long list of propositions to consider—in November 1988, there were 29 separate state propositions on the ballot! Although each proposal is briefly summarized, the language is often so technical and dense that voters can be easily misled. An additional criticism of direct democracy is that it sometimes wins majority support for proposals that are later declared unconstitutional. In reference to the recall, critics suggest that it can be used unfairly against a competent but unpopular official.

While such criticisms have much merit, the defenders of the initiative, referendum, and recall point out that in spite of flaws these mechanisms bring us closer to the spirit of democracy than our representative democracy (or republic) does. In some sense direct democracy adds a fourth element to the checks and balances of the three branches of government, one in which the voters themselves find a voice.

Reference Notes

1. John H. Culver and John C. Syer, *Power and Politics in California*, third edition, Macmillan, 1988, p. 143.
2. *Los Angeles Herald Examiner*, September 26, 1987, p. F-1.
3. Daniel C. Carson, "Sewage Pollution Threatens Southern California", *California Journal*, August 1985.
4. *Los Angeles Herald Examiner*, November 1, 1982, p. Al.
5. Mervin Field, "Will Independents Vote in Partisan Primaries?", *California Journal*, February 1987, p. 103.
6. Field Research Corporation Poll, as cited in *Los Angeles Times*, February 2, 1974.

8

The California Legislature

The California legislative branch is a bicameral body consisting of a forty-member senate elected for a four-year term and an eighty-member assembly elected for two. Half of the senators and the entire assembly are elected in November of even-numbered years.

Because each senate and each assembly district must be equal in population, the senate districts encompass twice as many residents as the assembly districts. Thus, the position of state senator is generally considered to be a more prestigious post than that of state assembly member.

Reapportionment and Gerrymandering

Every ten years (normally, the year following each census) the legislature must reapportion seats in both the senate and assembly—that is, the district boundaries must be redrawn to equalize district populations. This reapportionment may involve a manipulation of boundaries (known as *gerrymandering*) to benefit particular individuals and groups and to increase the strength of whichever party has a majority in the legislature. Partisan battling over district lines is fierce and often takes precedence over other important legislative business.

In 1981, because the Democrats held the legislative majority, they were able to shape the reapportionment in their favor. After the reapportionment bill was signed into law, Republicans were furious at the partisan advantage the gerrymandered boundaries had given the Democrats. Their attempts to overturn the boundaries and get new ones drawn included a referendum (June 1982) and several initiatives, all of which failed. After yet another unsuccessful effort through the judicial system, the Republicans gave up on trying to undo the 1981 boundaries and concentrated on trying to win enough legislative seats to get a majority for 1990.

Districts in which the incumbent does not hold a strong majority are known as *marginal*. Since the party that controls the legislature in 1990–1991 will determine the district lines for that decade (subject, however, to possible gubernatorial veto), both parties fight increasingly expensive election battles over each and every marginal district. It is well to remember that this battle for power also affects which party dominates California's federal congressional delegation, since the legislature draws the boundary lines for California's congressional districts. Because the state's population is growing more rapidly than the national average, California's seats in the House of Representatives will probably jump from 45 in the 1980s to 48 or 49 during the 1990s, thereby creating additional reapportionment opportunities.

Legislative Functions and Procedures

Unlike Congress, which has complete legislative power in the national government, the California legislature must share lawmaking power with the voters through the initiative and referendum processes described earlier. Nonetheless, state government policy is set primarily by the legislature. In addition, it has the "power of the purse," levying taxes and appropriating money to finance the operation of all state agencies. After the passage of Proposition 13 (June 1978), the legislature provided a large percentage of local government revenue as well.

The powers of the Senate and Assembly are nearly identical, although only the approval of the senate is needed to confirm certain administrative appointments by the governor. A member of either house can introduce any bill, and a majority of the entire membership of both houses is needed to pass most legislation (see Figure 8.1). A two-thirds majority is required for money bills, proposed constitutional amendments, and for urgency measures, which, unlike most laws, take effect immediately rather than January 1 of the following year.

Presiding Officers

The lieutenant governor is the presiding officer, or president, of the senate. In that capacity, however, he or she has little power and can vote only in cases of a tie. The person with greatest influence in the

Figure 8.1 *Passage of a law*

Initial Steps By Author

IDEA

Sources of bills; legislators, legislative committees, governor, state and local governmental agencies, business firms, lobbyists, citizens.

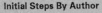

DRAFTING

Formal copy of bill and "layman's digest" prepared by Legislative Counsel.

INTRODUCTION

Bill submitted by senator or Assembly member. Numbered and read for the first time. Assigned to committee by Assembly or Senate Rules Committee. Printed.

Action in House of Origin

COMMITTEE

Testimony taken from author, proponents and opponents. Typical actions: Do pass; amend and do pass; no action; hold in com-mittee (kill); amend and re-refer to same committee; refer to another committee; send to interim study.
Bills with any fiscal implications, if approved by olicy committee, are referred to Appropriations Committee in the Senate and to Ways and Means Committee in the Assembly.

SECOND READING

Bills given do pass recommendations are read a second time and placed on file for debate

FLOOR DEBATE AND VOTE

Bills are read a third time and debated. A roll-call vote follows. For ordinary bills, 21 votes are needed in the Senate and 41 in the Assembly. For urgency bills and appropriation measures, 27 and 54 votes are required. If these numbers are not reached, the bill is defeated. Any member may seek reconsideration and a second vote. If passed with amendments, the bill is sent to the second house.

Disposition in Second House

READING

Bill is read for the first time and referred to committee by the Assembly or Senate Rules Committee.

COMMITTEE

Procedures and possible actions are identical to those in the first house.

SECOND READING

If cleared by committee, the bill is read a second time and placed on the daily file (agenda) for debate and vote.

SECOND READING

The procedure is identical to the first house. If a bill is passed without having been amended in the second house, it is sent to the governor's desk. (Resolutions are sent to the secretary of state's office.)

Resolution of Two-house Differences (if necessary)

CONCURRENCE

The house of origin decides whether to accept the second-house amendments. If the amendments are approved, the bill is sent to the governor. If the amendments are rejected, the bill is placed in the hands of a two-house conference committee composed of three senators and three Assembly members.

CONFERENCE

If the conferees fail to agree, the bill dies. If the conferees present a recommendation for compromise (conference report), both houses vote on the report. If the report is adopted by both, the bill goes to the governor. If either house rejects the report, a second (and even a third) conference committee can be formed.

Role of the Governor

SIGN OR VETO?

Within 12 days after receiving a bill, the governor can sign it into law, allow it to become law without his signature or veto it. A vetoed bill returns to the house of origin for possible vote on overriding the veto. It requires a two-thirds majority of both houses to override.

Urgency measures become effective immediately after signing. Others usually take effect the following January 1st.

Source: California Department of Finance.

senate is usually the *president pro tem*, a senator elected as a substitute presiding officer by the entire senate, and who becomes automatically the chair of the powerful Senate Rules Committee.

The presiding officer of the Assembly is known as the *speaker*, elected by all members of that body. The speaker's immense powers far exceed those of his or her counterparts in Congress or the state senate and include the authority to appoint and remove all committee chairs and members, to influence the referral of all bills to committees, and to serve as an ex-officio member of each committee. Usually the speakership has been won by the candidate favored by the majority party in the assembly, while in the senate the vote for president pro tem has sometimes crossed party lines.

Committees

As in Congress, all members of the legislature serve on at least one *standing committee*. Most members of the assembly serve on three committees and most senators on four or five. Each bill to come before the legislature is referred to the appropriate committee and is considered by it in an order usually determined by the chairperson. Most bills that fail to become law are killed in committee; those enacted have often been amended there before being considered on the floor of the senate or assembly where they may be further amended.

In marked contrast to the situation in Congress, committee appointments in the state legislature are not determined by seniority, and the chairs of various committees are often chosen from members of both parties. In the senate, the power to organize committees and appoint their members is vested in the Rules Committee, made up of the president pro tem (Los Angeles Democrat David Roberti since 1980) and four other senators also elected by the whole senate. In addition to the Rules committee, among the most important are the Education, Budget and Fiscal Review, Revenue and Taxation, Judiciary, and Health and Welfare Committees.

In the assembly, committees are appointed by the speaker. Among the most important is the Ways and Means Committee, which, like the Senate Budget and Fiscal Review Committee, considers all bills that involve the annual budget. Other important assembly committees are the Finance and Insurance, Education, Agriculture, and Transportation Committees.

If either house adds an amendment to a bill that is unacceptable to the house that first passed it, a *conference committee* consisting of three senators and three assembly members attempts to reach a compromise acceptable to both houses. When a bill is finally passed in the same form by both houses, it is sent to the governor to be signed.

The amount of partisanship in the legislature fluctuates. Sometimes internal battles within a party can be more disruptive than the battles between the two parties. The so-called "Gang of Five" dissident Democrats caused enormous tension and uncertainty in the Assembly in their unsuccessful 1988 efforts to oust Speaker Willie Brown, a fellow Democrat. Brown, the first black to hold the speakership, broke all previous records for tenure in the position when he completed his eighth year in 1988. Naturally, the more united party can try to take advantage of any divisions in the other party, but even then, the individual personalities and concerns of the legislators may prevent true unification from occurring within a party. With rare exceptions, however, the California legislature's Republicans and Democrats have divided more consistently along conservative and liberal lines than have their counterparts in Congress.

Since 1972, the legislature has met in two-year sessions. Although individuals of a similar calibre and ambition would generally earn a good deal more in the private sector, the legislators' base salaries ($37,105 per year plus an $87 daily allowance and a state car while the legislature is in session), adequate office facilities, and large number of staff assistants have attracted the kinds of men and women who have given it a reputation as one of the finest state legislatures in the nation. Unfortunately, scandals such as the 1988 FBI investigation into possible corruption of several legislators through the use of "honorariums" in exchange for legislative favors have somewhat diminished this image.

Despite enormous workloads and the pressures of frequent reelection campaigns, the state legislature manages to complete and pass hundreds of laws every session. Some of those enacted in the late 1980s include the outlawing of corporal punishment in public schools, requiring payroll deductions for child support payments, increasing the penalties for drunk driving and for air polluting, and requiring developers to pay fees towards school construction. Ongoing legislative battles involve such items as whether or not surrogate motherhood should be legal, the amount of state funds used for child care, whether toy guns that look like real firearms should be banned, and whether or not the state should invest in a "gamblers' special" high speed train between Southern California and Las Vegas.

9

The California Executive

California voters elect eight statewide executive officials, of whom the governor is obviously the most important. The governor acts as the ceremonial head of state, representing it at various formal and informal functions, and has considerable influence over the selection of the chair of his or her party's state central committee. In the total system of checks and balances among the three branches of government, the governor exercises the executive checks. The most important of these is the *veto* power, especially when used on bills appropriating money.

The Governor's Budget and the Veto Power

When the legislature passes a bill, the governor has twelve days in which to veto it by sending it back to the legislature or to sign it into law. If he or she does neither, the bill becomes law automatically. While about 8 percent of all laws have been vetoed in recent times, the legislature only rarely can amass the two-thirds vote necessary to override a veto.

Each year the governor must send a budget bill to the legislature providing for the expenditure of specified funds for all government agencies. Although the bill may be frequently amended before it is passed and returned to the governor, he or she may then use what is known as the *item veto*. This permits the deletion of a particular expenditure or the reduction of its amount, thereby giving the governor more formal control over state finances than the president can exert at the national level. Governor Deukmejian has made extensive use of the item veto and has drastically cut such items as funding for the California Coastal Commission, the California Occupational Safety and Health Administration, bilingual education, and AIDS research.[1] Despite the controversial nature of some of his vetoes, as a Republican governor with a Democratic-controlled legislature, he has been remarkably successful in avoiding legislative *overrides* of his decisions (Table 9.1).

Other Checks

The governor's other checks on the legislative branch include sending messages to suggest new legislation and the authority to call special sessions. One of the more important ceremonial, and political, moments for a governor is the annual "State of the State" speech given before the legislature and other constitutional officers. In this address, the governor indicates what issues the legislators should work on while attempting to give an upbeat picture of California's economic and social status. Ideas presented here can then be introduced into the assembly or senate by the governor's allies in those bodies.

The governor's greatest influence on the judicial branch is the power to appoint a good number of judges (see the discussion of this procedure in the next chapter.) In addition, the governor may exercise executive clemency, which consists of pardons, commutations (reductions of sentences), and reprieves (postponements of sentences) granted to convicts. For those with past felony records, however, pardons and commutations require the approval of a majority on the state supreme court.

Military and Police Power

The governor is the commander in chief of the California National Guard (unless the president has placed it under federal control) and may call it into active duty in emergencies such as large-scale social disturbances or natural disasters. He or she may also direct the highway patrol to bolster local police and sheriff's officers if intervention is needed on a smaller scale.

Table 9.1 *California's governors*

Peter H. Burnett	Democrat	1849-1851
John McDougal (acting)	Democrat	1851-1852
John Bigler	Democrat	1852-1856
John N. Johnson	Know-Nothing	1856-1858
John B. Weller	Democrat	1858-1860
Milton S. Latham	Democrat	1860
John G. Downey (acting)	Democrat	1860-1861
Leland Stanford	Republican	1861-1863
Frederick F. Low	Union	1863-1867
Henry H. Haight	Democrat	1867-1871
Newton Booth	Republican	1871-1875
Romualdo Pacheco (acting)	Republican	1875
William Irwin	Democrat	1875-1880
George C. Perkins	Republican	1880-1883
George Stoneman	Democrat	1883-1887
Washington Bartlett	Democrat	1887
Robert W. Waterman (acting)	Republican	1887-1891
Henry H. Markham	Republican	1891-1895
James H. Budd	Democrat	1895-1899
Henry T. Gage	Republican	1899-1903
George C. Pardee	Republican	1903-1907
James N. Gillette	Republican	1907-1911
Hiram W. Johnson	Republican	1911-1917
William D. Stephens	Republican	1917-1923
Friend W. Richardson	Republican	1923-1927
C.C. Young	Republican	1927-1931
James Rolph, Jr.	Republican	1931-1934
Frank C. Merriam	Republican	1934-1939
Culbert L. Olson	Democrat	1939-1943
Earl Warren	Republican	1943-1953
Goodwin J. Knight	Republican	1953-1959
Edmund G. Brown	Democrat	1959-1967
Ronald Reagan	Republican	1967-1975
Edmund G. Brown, Jr.	Democrat	1975-1983
George Deukmejian	Republican	1983-

Source: *Los Angeles County Almanac*, 1988, p. 79. Reprinted by permission of the L.A. County Republican Central Committee.

Administrative Responsibility

The governor discharges the obligation to enforce state laws through a vast administrative bureaucracy consisting of about fifty departments, most of which are currently grouped within five huge agencies: Business, Transportation and Housing; Health and Welfare;

Resources; State and Consumer Services, and Youth and Adult Corrections (see Figure 9.1). The heads of these agencies, in addition to the directors of the Departments of Finance, Food and Agriculture, and Industrial Relations, constitute the governor's cabinet and are appointed by the governor, subject to senate confirmation. The finance director is responsible for preparing the entire state budget for submission to the legislature. Like most governors, Governor Deukmejian has had occasional problems getting his first-choice nominees confirmed by the state senate.

The governor also has major responsibilities in connection with several administrative boards, four of which are in the field of education. He generally appoints the members with the concurrence of the state senate. Among these are:

1. the Board of Regents, which governs the various branches of the University of California and consists of the governor, several other ex-officio members, and members appointed by the governor for twelve-year terms.
2. the Board of Trustees of the California State Colleges and Universities, sixteen of whose twenty-four members are appointed by the governor for eight-year terms and of which the governor is also a member.
3. the sixteen-member Board of Governors of the California Community Colleges, appointed by the governor for four-year terms to coordinate the locally controlled community college districts.
4. the Board of Education, the ten members of which are appointed by the governor for four-year terms to make the policy for public schools throughout the state on such matters as curriculum and textbook adoption.
5. the five-member state Personnel Board, appointed by the governor for ten-year terms, which supervises the civil service system encompassing 98 percent of all state employees.
6. the five-person Public Utilities Commission, appointed by the governor for six-year terms, which licenses more than 1500 privately owned companies and regulates the rates charged and services provided in the gas, water, telephone, telegraph, electricity, and transportation industries.
7. the five-member Energy Commission, created in 1974 and appointed by the governor for the purpose of approving the construction of power plants and fixing efficiency standards for heating and lighting systems as well as for home appliances.

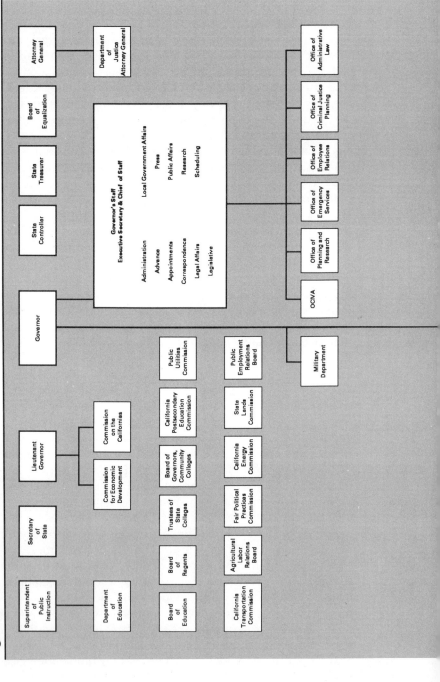

Figure 9.1 The Executive Branch California State Government

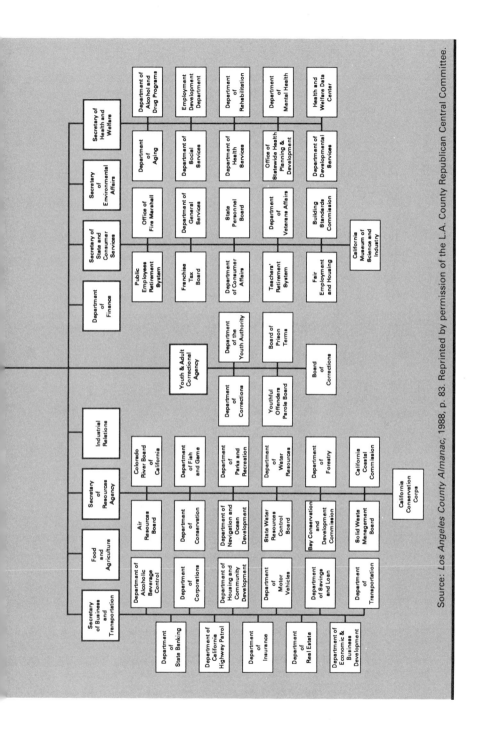

Source: *Los Angeles County Almanac,* 1988, p. 83. Reprinted by permission of the L.A. County Republican Central Committee.

8. the seven-member Fair Employment and Housing Commission, appointed by the governor, with responsibility for prohibiting both job and housing discrimination.
9. the Workers' Compensation Appeals Board, also consisting of seven members appointed by the governor, which settles disputes regarding money paid to employees suffering job-related injuries or illness.
10. the California Adult Authority, whose eight members are appointed by the governor to determine which male convicts should be granted parole from state prisons.
11. the five-member Public Employment Relations Board, which regulates collective bargaining involving unions of workers employed by the state government, the University of California, California state colleges and universities, community colleges, and public schools.

Occasionally, appointees for some of the above-mentioned commissions become highly controversial. Betty Cordoba, nominated by Governor Deukmejian for the Public Employment Relations Board and known for her criticisms of collective bargaining for public workers, was rejected by the Senate after an intensive lobbying effort by the labor movement.

The governor also has the authority to appoint replacements to fill vacancies on County Boards of Supervisors, as well as those occurring for any of the seven other executive officers and for California's U.S. Senators.

The Plural Executive

In addition to the governor, seven other executive officials are directly elected by the voters. Like the governor, they are chosen for four-year terms and hold the following positions, often known as *constitutional offices:*

1. The lieutenant governor, in addition to being nominal President of the state senate, succeeds to the governorship if that office becomes vacant between elections. The lieutenant governor also serves as acting governor when the governor is out of the state.

    It is this situation, perhaps more than any other, that discouraged George Deukmejian from considering the Republican vice presidential nomination in 1988. Since the Lieutenant Governor was Democrat Leo McCarthy, if Deukmejian had left the governorship, he would have turned the state over to the opposition party. This system in which the second-in-command may be from a different party than the governor has been criticized for permitting such issues to arise and some observers have suggested that the governor and lieutenant governor should run on a ticket much as the president and vice-president do.

2. The attorney general, the chief legal adviser to all state agencies, is also head of the state Justice Department. This department provides assistance to local law enforcement agencies, represents the state in lawsuits, and exercises supervision over the county district attorneys in their prosecution of state criminal defendants. Three governors—Earl Warren, Edmund G. (Pat) Brown, and George Deukmejian—had served previously as attorney general. In 1986, John Van de Kamp of Los Angeles was reelected to the post, placing him in a good position for the 1990 gubernatorial race.

3. The controller is concerned with government finance. He or she audits state expenditures, supervises financial restrictions on local governments, and influences state tax collections as a member of the Board of Equalization. Moreover, the controller has considerable patronage power in appointing inheritance tax appraisers and is a member of the State Lands Commission, which oversees the state's 4 million acres of public lands. He or she is also chair of the Franchise Tax Board, which collects income taxes. The office of controller, like attorney general, may also serve as a stepping stone to higher office. It has been no secret that Gray Davis intends to use it for that purpose in the 1990s.

4. The California secretary of state maintains official custody over state legal documents, grants charters to business corporations, and administers state election procedures. One of the most important tasks of the secretary of state is to verify the signatures on petitions for ballot initiatives, referendums, and recalls. March Fong Eu, after a brief 1987 attempt to run for the Democratic nomination for the U.S. Senate, remained to serve her fourth term as Secretary of State.

5. Although the office of state treasurer has usually been a dead end politically in California, it entails serious responsibilities. The treasurer maintains custody over tax money collected by various state agencies, deposits it in private banks until appropriated by the legislature, and sells government bonds, presumably at the lowest possible interest rate, when the state is au-

thorized to borrow money. Jesse Unruh, who had been one of the most powerful speakers in the history of the assembly, wielded the powers of Treasurer with great finesse until his death in 1987. His influence over the investment of state pension funds gave him a significant role in stock and bond markets.

6. The five executive officers listed above are, like the governor, nominated and elected through partisan campaigns. Candidates for superintendent of public instruction, however, are elected on a nonpartisan basis, without party designation listed on the ballot. The superintendent of public instruction directs the state Department of Education and is charged with the responsibility of dispensing financial aid to local school districts, granting teaching credentials, and enforcing policies determined by the state Board of Education. In addition, the superintendent is an *ex-officio* member of the Board of Regents and the Board of Trustees. Bill Honig, reelected to his second term in 1986, has become known for his combative style and willingness to challenge the governor over budget allocations for education. He has also spearheaded citizen movements to qualify initiatives such as Proposition 98 (November 1988) for the ballot. This proposition, which passed by 51 percent to 49 percent, proposed that a fixed percentage of the state's budget be spent on public school and community college education every year.

7. Beginning in 1990, the stated insurance commissioner will also be elected.

In addition to the constitutional executive officers just mentioned, California voters choose four members of the Board of Equalization from the four districts into which the state is divided for this purpose. This board collects the sales tax, a major source of state revenue, and equalizes the basis on which local property taxes are assessed.

One of the most frequently criticized characteristics of state government is the election of so many executive officials. The voters have little information about the candidates seeking these offices and the governor cannot coordinate their activities effectively. This problem is particularly acute when some of the constitutional officers are not in the governor's party or are even potential future rivals for the governorship.

Reference Notes

1. *Los Angeles Times*, July 9, 1988 Part I, p. 20.

10

The California Courts

The courts comprising the judicial branch of California's state government have been widely praised throughout the country. Not only have they established legal principles later followed by the United States Supreme Court, but they have been organized since 1950 in what has been considered an unusually simple and efficient system. Nevertheless, the state's high crime rates and substantial amounts of litigation have led many observers to worry about the "overload" in the judicial system that causes much delay and expense for all concerned. Four levels of courts comprise this vast and vital branch of California government (see Figure 10.1).

Municipal and Justice Courts

At the lowest level are the 85 municipal courts, serving judicial districts with over 40,000 people, and 89 justice courts, serving less populated areas. These *inferior courts*, as they are sometimes called, decide such matters as small claims cases for up to $1500 in which no attorney is involved, and civil suits asking less than $25,000 in damages. Thus, the inferior courts minimize costs and reach speedy decisions. In addition, they hear the less important criminal cases (misdemeanors) and hold preliminary hearings regarding major crimes (felonies).

Superior Courts

Each of California's fifty-eight counties has a superior court, in the larger counties including dozens of judges. They have appellate jurisdiction enabling them to hear cases from municipal and justice

Figure 10.1 California's court system

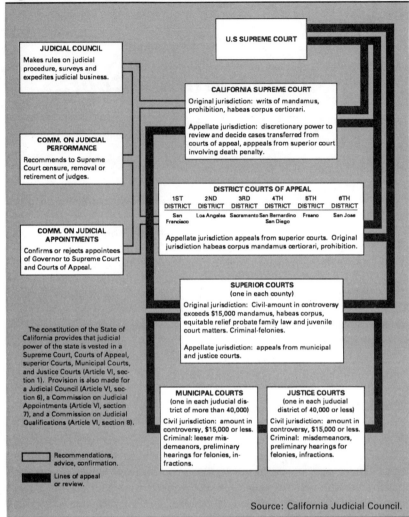

JUDICIAL COUNCIL

Makes rules on judicial procedure, surveys and expedites judicial business.

U.S SUPREME COURT

CALIFORNIA SUPREME COURT

Original jurisdiction: writs of mandamus, prohibition, habeas corpus certiorari.

Appellate jurisdiction: discretionary power to review and decide cases transferred from courts of appeal, apppeals from superior court involving death penalty.

COMM. ON JUDICIAL PERFORMANCE

Recommends to Supreme Court censure, removal or retirement of judges.

DISTRICT COURTS OF APPEAL

1ST DISTRICT	2ND DISTRICT	3RD DISTRICT	4TH DISTRICT	5TH DISTRICT	6TH DISTRICT
San Francisco	Los Angeles	Sacramento	San Bernardino San Diego	Fresno	San Jose

Appellate jurisdiction appeals from superior courts. Original jurisdiction habeas corpus mandamus certiorari, prohibition.

COMM. ON JUDICIAL APPOINTMENTS

Confirms or rejects appointees of Governor to Supreme Court and Courts of Appeal.

SUPERIOR COURTS
(one in each county)

Original jurisdiction: Civil-amount in controversy exceeds $15,000 mandamus, habeas corpus, equitable relief probate family law and juvenile court matters. Criminal-felonies.

Appellate jurisdiction: appeals from municipal and justice courts.

The constitution of the State of California provides that judicial power of the state is vested in a Supreme Court, Courts of Appeal, superior Courts, Municipal Courts, and Justice Courts (Article VI, section 1). Provision is also made for a Judicial Council (Article VI, section 6), a Commission on Judicial Appointments (Article VI, section 7), and a Commission on Judicial Qualifications (Article VI, section 8).

MUNICIPAL COURTS
(one in each judicial district of more than 40,000)

Civil jurisdiction: amount in controversy, $15,000 or less. Criminal: leeser misdemeanors, preliminary hearings for felonies, infractions.

JUSTICE COURTS
(one in each judicial district of 40,000 or less)

Civil jurisdiction: amount in controversy, $15,000 or less. Criminal: misdemeanors, preliminary hearings for felonies, infractions.

☐ Recommendations, advice, confirmation.

■ Lines of appeal or review.

Source: California Judicial Council.

courts on appeal, as well as original jurisdiction over civil cases involving $25,000 or more, felonies, all juvenile cases, and all dissolution of marriage cases. They are the major trial courts in California.

District Courts of Appeal

California is divided into six court of appeal districts, headquartered in San Francisco, Los Angeles, Sacramento, Fresno, San Jose, and one maintaining offices in both San Bernardino and San Diego. These courts have appellate jurisdiction only, hearing appeals from lower tribunals. Three judges hear each case.

California Supreme Court

The original jurisdiction of the supreme court is limited to issuance of a few court orders, or writs, with the vast bulk of its cases coming to it on appeal from lower courts. It consists of a chief justice, receiving $98,728 per year, and six associate justices, who get $94,147. These salaries are generally higher than those received by any other state court judges in the nation (except for Alaska),[1] although fairly low compared with the incomes of most successful attorneys in private practice.

The Selection of Judges

Judges on the justice, municipal, and superior courts are chosen by the voters in nonpartisan elections for six-year terms. No one may become a judge who has not been a lawyer for at least five years. A majority of judges are unopposed when they seek reelection and even those who run with opposition rarely lose. However, vacancies occur between elections due to death, retirement, and the creation of additional judgeships by the legislature in an attempt to keep up with the steady increase in the number of cases. These vacancies permit governors to appoint many new judges to serve until the next election, at which time these incumbents usually retain their offices.

In making judicial appointments, governors usually give top consideration to attorneys who have supported their last political campaign and who have a good reputation with the local bar association. Unlike Jerry Brown, who nominated record numbers of women and minorities to the bench, George Deukmejian's 500 or so judicial nominees include a preponderance of white males who had been government attorneys, primarily prosecutors.[2] In general, private attorneys earn much higher incomes than judges and thus are rarely interested in judicial positions until late in their careers.

Judges on the district courts of appeals and the supreme court are chosen in a method designed to combine the advantages of both appointment and election, which involves the following three-step process:

1. appointment by the governor;
2. confirmation by the Commission on Judicial Appointments, which consists of a supreme court judge, a district court of appeals judge, and the state attorney general;
3. election for a twelve-year term, with no opposing candidate permitted to run and voters limited to a choice between "yes" and "no."

Perhaps the most controversial battle ever waged over the appointment, confirmation, and retention of a California justice was that regarding Rose Elizabeth Bird. Rose Bird was nominated by then-Governor Jerry Brown in 1977, barely approved by the Commission on Judicial Appointments with a 2-1 vote, and then, after nearly losing the seat in her 1978 confirmation election, was voted out of office in the confirmation election of 1986. It was that year that the state supreme court experienced its most traumatic upheaval at the polls: voters rejected not only Chief Justice Bird but also removed Associate Justices Cruz Reynoso (the first Latino to sit on the high court) and Joseph Grodin. The unseating of three supreme court justices left many Californians concerned about the proper balance between the voters' rights to participate in government and the judicial branch's need to remain impartial and protected from the current political mood.

The Removal of Judges

In addition to the electorate's decisions about which judges to retain and which to remove from office, the Commission on Judicial Performance is another avenue by which judges can be ousted from office. Formed in 1969, the Commission is made up of five judges appointed by the supreme court, two attorneys chosen by the

California Bar Association, and two nonlawyers appointed by the governor. Its primary task is to investigate complaints about judicial misconduct and, if circumstances indicate, to recommend that the state supreme court remove a judge from office.

Since its inception, the Commission has looked into hundreds of complaints, issuing some 53 private admonitions, and recommending the removal of five judges and the official censure of thirteen others. However, the investigation itself often solves the problem: approximately seventy judges have seen fit to retire or resign while under the Commission's scrutiny. Causes for investigation do not include judicial policies but rather focus on actual breaches of propriety such as excessive drinking, frequent tardiness, verbal abuse, ethnic or sexual disparagements, or disability caused by poor health or aging.

The Judicial Council

The virtues of the California court system, such as they are, may be attributed largely to the judicial council. This group keeps abreast of problems in the judicial branch and recommends court reorganization plans and the creation of additional judgeships to the legislature. Additionally, it makes rules for judicial procedure and, if needed, transfers judges from one court to another. Chaired by the chief justice of the supreme court, the judicial council consists of twenty-one persons, including fifteen judges from all levels of the court system, four practicing attorneys, and two members of the legislature.

Judicial Review and Judicial Politics

In addition to settling disputes between residents and convicting criminals, the California courts, like others in the nation, exercise the power of judicial review. In the hands of state judges, this is a "double" power, permitting them to declare government acts invalid because they violate either the U.S. or state constitution. Because the cases brought to the state supreme court are often the most controversial and complex, and because the decisions made at this level can only be revoked by the U.S. supreme court, understanding the political composition of the state supreme court is of great importance in understanding the nature of law in California.

When governors appoint supreme court justices, they hope to have their choices confirmed not only initially but for years to come when the voters exercise their confirmation rights. Thus, they select justices whose overall political views are compatible with their own, and expect that these justices will make legal decisions that conform to their judgment. Nevertheless, once on the high bench, many appointees disappoint the governors who put them there by making decisions contrary to the wishes of their "patrons."

Even Governor Duekmejian, who was able to appoint a total of five of the seven state supreme court justices by 1988, had to suffer such a disappointment when the Court ruled against him in the matter of Dan Lungren's contested nomination for state treasurer. Despite his dissatisifaction with the ruling, the Governor understood that the independent nature of the judiciary required him to obey the decision and select a new nominee.

Given the conservative views of the governor and his five appointees, Californians are now in an era in which the court generally favors business interests, strict punishment for criminals, and the reinstatement of the death penalty in the state. Additionally, the court has already made controversial decisions involving the use of Medi-cal monies for abortions, the propriety of local roadblocks being set up to make random checks for drunk drivers, and the legality of adult-only mobile home parks.

Even with the complex nature of the issues they face, the seven state supreme court justices may tend to think similarly not only because so many of them were appointed by the same governor but also because they share such similar backgrounds. All but one are middle-aged males who have been judges nearly all their professional lives, and none have served in the legal aid or public defenders' offices where more liberal lawyers tend to congregate.[3] Nevertheless, betting on Court decisions is not a very profitable activity—no matter who serves, the Court as an institution is seldom completely predictable.

Reference Notes

1. *Los Angeles Times*, August 28, 1978, p. 16 and USA Today, July 2, 1984, p. 4A.
2. *Los Angeles Times*, July 6, 1988, Part II, p. 8.
3. *California Journal*, June 1988, p. 240.

11

Criminal Justice and Civil Law

All the vast machinery of the judicial system and its related components, including the judges, attorneys, bailiffs, stenographers, police, jails, wardens, and parole officers (to name a few), serves to facilitate two basic types of legal procedures: either civil litigation or criminal proceedings. Although many Californians' maximum contact with the entire judicial/legal system is their occasional jury duty, for others their lives are profoundly affected by the structures and processes of the criminal justice system and/or civil trials.

Criminal Justice

Depending on the severity of the act, crimes are normally defined as either felonies, misdemeanors, or infractions. *Infractions* are most often violations of traffic laws while *misdemeanors* encompass "less serious" crimes like shoplifting and public drunkenness. *Felonies*, the most serious crimes and potentially punishable by a year or more in state prison, are tried in superior courts, while the other two categories are handled by municipal courts (see Table 11.1 and 11.2).

Californians, through both the initiative process and their elected officials, have shown an increasing concern about how to properly punish convicted criminals. In 1978, voters passed Proposition 8, the "Victim's Bill of Rights," which reduced the possibility of bail for the accused and created stiffer punishments for the convicted. The same year, they also passed an initiative allowing the use of the death penalty under "special circumstances."

Table 11.1 *Number of felony arrests by offense 1982-1984*

	1982		1983		1984	
Crime	Number	Percent	Number	Percent	Number	Percent
Violent Crimes						
Homicide	3,665	4%	3,495	5%	3,896	5%
Rape	4,443	5	4,382	6	4,369	6
Robbery	27,072	33	23,883	32	23,109	30
Assault	44,154	54	40,948	55	43,145	56
Kidnapping	2,260	3	2,190	3	2,224	3
Total Violent Crimes	81,594	100%	74,898	100%	76,743	100%
Property Crimes						
Burglary	86,921	47%	80,917	48%	76,295	46%
Theft	59,908	32	52,486	31	51,144	31
Motor Vehicle Theft	23,509	13	22,300	13	23,108	14
Forgery	12,912	7	12,226	7	12,138	7
Arson	1,893	1	1,884	1	2,066	1
Total Property Crimes	185,143	100%	169,813	100%	164,752	100%
Drug Law Violations						
Narcotics	NA	NA	31,588	40%	42,479	46%
Marijuana	NA	NA	19,920	25	21,350	23
Dangerous Drugs	NA	NA	25,302	32	27,820	30
Other	NA	NA	79,422	100%	93,124	100%
Total Drug Law Violations	NA	NA	79,422	100%	93,124	100%
All Other Felony Arrests	NA	—	49,476	—	50,243	—
Total Felony Arrests	NA	—	373,609	—	384,861	—

Source: California Dept. of Justice *Crime and Delinquency in California*, 1984.

Despite the passage of the 1978 initiative, executions were delayed in California for more than ten years. Although lower courts have sentenced over two hundred convicted criminals to death, all of them are entitled to an automatic appeal to the state supreme court. During the years that Rose Bird was Chief Justice, only three of the death penalty decisions were affirmed by the court (the executions did not occur because of further appeals to the federal courts).[1] Because opinion polls in California have shown a steady rise in public support for capital punishment,[2] the public's anger at the Bird court for not applying the death penalty became the theme of the 1986 campaign to oust Bird and two of her colleagues. Under Chief Justice Malcolm Lucas, the court, dominated by Deukmejian appointees, has undertaken to review numerous death penalty cases as quickly as possible and it has upheld capital punishments at about a four to one ratio.[3]

Table 11.2 Number of misdemeanor arrests by offense 1982–1984

Crime	1982 Number	1982 Percent	1983 Number	1983 Percent	1984 Number	1984 Percent
Assault and Battery	56,746	4%	57,557	4%	59,681	5%
Petty Theft	124,597	10	119,149	9	117,803	9
Checks and Credit Cards	2,013	*	2,150	*	1,814	*
Drug Law Violations	82,612	6	106,458	8	117,119	9
Indecent Exposure	2,822	*	3,013	*	3,206	*
Annoying Children	671	*	599	*	617	*
Obscene Matter	33	*	56	*	50	*
Lewd Conduct	6,175	*	7,171	*	8,166	*
Prostitution	15,929	1	16,562	1	20,015	2
Drunk	231,031	18	227,506	18	217,488	17
Disorderly Conduct	10,546	*	10,322	*	12,557	1
Disturbing the Peace	15,873	1	15,068	1	14,878	1
Driving under the Influence	338,344	27	346,267	27	345,497	26
Hit-and-run	5,329	*	6,053	*	6,730	*
Traffic-custody	140,976	11	138,429	11	143,474	11
Gambling	2,627	*	2,174	*	1,968	*
Nonsupport	805	*	790	*	779	*
All Other	179,092	14	188,945	15	243,415	19
Total	1,271,245	100%	1,294,418	100%	1,312,370	100%

*Less than one percent.
Source: California Department of Justice, *Crime and Delinquency in California*, 1984.

In addition to the public mood calling for use of the death penalty, Californians seem eager for longer jail terms for noncapital crimes even when that choice leads to a serious prison overcrowding problem. The Board of Corrections has estimated approximately 62,300 jail inmates in the year 1990 at an annual operating cost of $1 billion.[4] Bond measures passed in 1988 help pay for additional building costs, but the problem of where to locate new prisons has produced a serious statewide political battle. The *NIMBY* (not in my backyard) syndrome is the typical response of most communities when told that a new prison is being considered for the area, and much legislative haggling, gubernatorial posturing, and citizen activism accompanies the discussion.

Crime and its Victims

Like many other states, California has its share of unemployment, family instability, hopelessness, and ignorance—the underlying causes of much of the crime committed in the state. Despite beefed-up law enforcement efforts, certain sections of some large cities are plagued by drug abuse and gang violence, often accompanied by related crimes such as automobile theft and residential burglaries (usually by drug addicts seeking quick money). Among the more tragic side effects of the gang/drug problems is the killing of innocent people (including children) who are in the wrong place at the wrong time or wearing a color combination with gang-related connotations. In their efforts to avoid the problems of gang shootings and drug dealings, smaller communities are trying novel approaches in prevention. The city of Rialto in San Bernardino County has considered a "gang assessment district" property tax that would cost the average homeowner an extra $24 per year and would raise enough money to hire seven additional police officers to create an anti-gang program.[5]

Although the emphasis on drug abuse as both a crime and a social problem has caused a 96.8 percent increase in arrests for drug violations between 1982 and 1987, the overall 1987 state crime rate dropped by 3.3 percent.[6] While this small decrease in crime is a hopeful note, serious problems remain unresolved, including the issues of school security, the high costs of trials, the rights of the accused, and the cost to society of living with an interminable fear of crime. Despite the state law requiring *restitution* for victims of crimes, few criminals are in a position to compensate their victims, and state funds for post-trauma counseling for crime victims depend on the willingness of politicians to support such services.

The Criminal Justice Process

In many cases, crimes occur and are not reported, or they are reported but no suspect is arrested. In the cases where an arrest is made, the arresting officer often has the option of "naming" the crime by labeling it either a misdemeanor or a felony. If a person is arrested for a felony, the district attorney's office must then decide whether to file the felony charge.

The final stage at which the fate of the accused is determined is at the time of sentencing. In jury trials, the twelve jurors must come to unanimous agreement regarding whether to acquit or convict the accused. *Plea bargaining*, the practice of arranging a lighter sentence in exchange for admitting guilt to a lesser crime, is still used about 90 percent of the time and eliminates the trial completely.

Civil Law

While criminal law deals with matters considered injurious to the "people of the state of California," civil matters entail any disputes between parties that cannot be resolved without legal assistance. Parties involved in such disputes can include individuals, business entities, and government agencies. The range of civil legal matters includes such cases as dissolution of marriage and child custody, personal injury, such as automobile accidents, malpractice, breach of contract, property disputes, and much more. In these cases, the court's role frequently is to determine liability and assess damages, often amounting to hundreds of thousands of dollars.

One of the most controversial areas of civil law today involves automobile accidents and insurance. Trial lawyers argue that there should be no limits on claims for damages (thus potentially expanding their own percentage-based fees) while insurance companies prefer a "no-fault" system in which medical and auto repair costs are covered regardless of who caused the accident.

Most civil lawsuits, like many criminal cases, never go to a full trial. In civil matters, out-of-court settlements arranged by the attorneys of the parties involved often save time, money, and aggravation for both the plaintiff and the defendant. However, if the plaintiff so desires, a civil matter may be tried with a full jury, but in such cases only a two-thirds majority is required to come to a conclusion. Because going to court has become a common method of resolving disputes, there is currently about a four-year wait in the large metropolitan areas of the state from the time a suit is filed to the time it can be heard in court.

Juries

California has two types of juries: grand juries and trial juries. Grand juries consist of nineteen people (twenty-three in Los Angeles County) who are nominated by county judges and selected by lottery. Their function is to investigate any possible problems in local government and to return *indictments,* or charges, against suspected lawbreakers. Grand juries are peculiar institutions in that they operate in secret and the accused may not have an attorney present nor may he or she cross-examine witnesses. For these reasons, the state supreme court ruled in 1978 that anyone indicted by a grand jury is entitled to a speedy preliminary hearing at which the customary rights of the defendant may be invoked.

Trial juries are composed of twelve citizens for a felony trial, but may be made up of fewer people for a misdemeanor case or a civil trial. After many years of relying on voter registration lists to contact Californians for jury duty, the state determined that these lists produced a disproportionately small number of ethnic minorities on juries. Today one of the lists used is that of the Department of Motor Vehicles, which includes all California's licensed drivers. Among long-standing problems with the jury system are the limited numbers of people who can afford to serve (most Californians earn $5 per day on the jury and forego their usual earnings while they serve), the tedium of waiting to be selected for a trial, and the potential for emotional, rather than rational, decisions on the part of the jurors. Despite these flaws, and periodic efforts to reduce the number of jurors needed for a trial, trial by a full jury remains an important option in California's judicial system.

Reference Notes

1. Daniel C. Carson, "Legislators Cut Through Execution Barriers", *California Government and Politics Annual*, 1986-87, edited by Thomas R. Hoeber and Charles M. Price, p. 44.
2. *Los Angeles Times*, August 19, 1985, p. 1, and Los Angeles Herald Examiner, April 3, 1985, p. 1.
3. *Los Angeles Times*, July 12, 1988, Part I, P. 18.
4. John H. Sullivan, "The Hidden Costs of Building New Jails," *California Government and Politics Annual*, 1986-1987, edited by Thomas R. Hoeber and Charles M. Price, p. 46.
5. *Los Angeles Times*, June 29, 1988, Part I, p. 1.
6. *Los Angeles Times*, July 9, 1988, Part I, p. 32.

12

City Governments

There are four units of local government in California—counties, cities, school districts, and other special districts. Since all fifty states are unitary, these local units have only the authority which the state government gives to them. Cities, especially, need all the power they can get, for they must cope with the worst crimes, pollution, and other problems to be found anywhere in the state.

How Cities are Created

With the exceptions of some of the older cities, such as Los Angeles, San Francisco, and San Jose, which received their charters from the state when California was admitted to the union, most cities in California "incorporate" when the residents decide they need their own local government. Residents of *unincorporated areas* normally receive basic services from the county in which they live. Occasionally, an unincorporated area is simply annexed, or added on, to a nearby city by a majority vote of that territory's residents, along with the approval of the adjacent city. However, incorporation is the most typical method by which citizens acquire a city government.

Perhaps the most common reason why residents initiate the process of incorporation is that the county government, which provides their services, is too far away and unresponsive. If residents feel that police and fire protection is inadequate, or that planning and zoning issues are not well handled, or even that rents are too high in the area, they may organize to create their own city in which they can elect their own officials to control these issues. Residents in Los Angeles County from Malibu to Diamond Bar recently organized incorporation efforts for just these sorts of reasons.

Incorporation begins with a petition to the Local Agency Formation Commission (LAFCO). LAFCO's task is to determine whether or not a city is viable—that is, whether or not it is going to be both economically solvent and able to provide the services it would no longer get from the county. With LAFCO's approval, the residents must then get signatures from at least 25 percent of the registered voters in the area or 25 percent of the landowners whose holdings equal at least one-fourth of the land within its boundaries. If this requirement is met, the issue is brought to the voters in the next election and can be approved by a simple majority. This process was followed successfully in West Hollywood and Santa Clarita, two of the cities incorporated in the mid 1980s.

City Responsibilities

Whether a city is a "general law" city that derives all its powers from statutes passed by the state legislature, or a "charter" city that has its own locally written constitution, all cities share similar tasks and responsibilities. Basic, day-to-day necessities such as sewage and garbage disposal, police and fire services, streets and traffic control, recreation and parks, and planning and zoning form the backbone of city services (Table 12.1). In a good number of cities formed since World War II, some of these services are provided through the so-called "Lakewood Plan" in which cities contract with the county to rent services such as police, fire protection, and street maintenance.

Forms of City Government

With many variations, city government in California falls within two broad types. The *mayor-council* variety entails a separation of powers between the mayor, who has responsibility for the functioning of most city departments, and the council, which enacts legislation known as *ordinances*. If the mayor has the power to veto ordinances and to appoint department heads, the government is known as a strong mayor-council variety; if not, it is a weak mayor-council system (see Figure 12.1).

Table 12.1 Selected revenue and expenditure figures for California's nine largest cities, 1985

City, Population (1986)	Intergovernmental Revenue per Capita[1]	Taxes per Capita[2]	Gross Debt Outstanding per Capita[2]	Total General Expenditure[3]	Housing and Community Development[3]	Police Protection[3]	Fire Protection[3]	Highways
Los Angeles, 3,097,000	$148	$373	$1,185	$1,940	$154	$422	$164	$97
San Diego, 1,015,000	153	220	1,132	504	53	81	37	30
San Francisco,[4] 749,000	904	791	1,949	1,353	49	116	62	10
San Jose, 712,000	123	311	744	416	35	58	34	86
Long Beach, 396,000	248	312	1,117	365	30	61	39	22
Oakland, 357,000	167	385	2,038	337	24	43	25	18
Sacramento, 324,000	87	295	414	165	3	37	24	22
Fresno, 285,000	128	244	599	145	3	30	14	16
Anaheim, 241,000	93	285	2,080	157	15	27	13	7

[1]From national and state governments.
[2]Based on 1984 population estimates.
[3]In millions of dollars.
[4]San Francisco in a combined city and county. As a result, its major expenditures included $263 million for health and hospitals and $164 million for public welfare.

Source: U.S. Bureau of the Census, *Statistical Abstract of the United States, 1988* (108th ed.), Washington, D.C., p. 33, 34, 277, 279.

Figure 12.1 Forms of city government

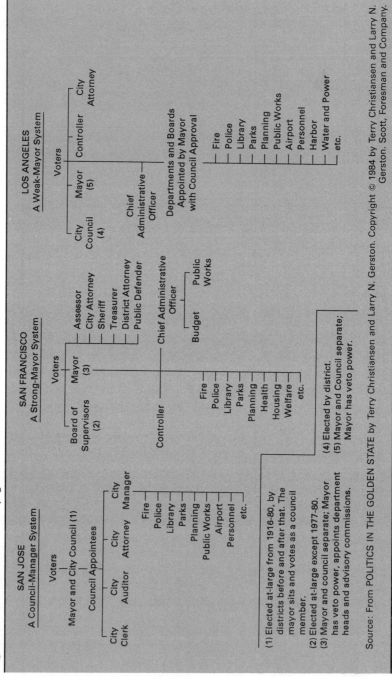

SAN JOSE
A Council-Manager System

Voters

Mayor and City Council (1)

Council Appointees

City Clerk — City Auditor — City Attorney — City Manager

Fire
Police
Library
Parks
Planning
Public Works
Airport
Personnel
etc.

SAN FRANCISCO
A Strong-Mayor System

Voters

Board of Supervisors (2) — Mayor (3)

Assessor
City Attorney
Sheriff
Treasurer
District Attorney
Public Defender

Controller — Chief Administrative Officer

Budget — Public Works

Fire
Police
Library
Parks
Planning
Health
Housing
Welfare
etc.

LOS ANGELES
A Weak-Mayor System

Voters

City Council (4) — Mayor (5) — Controller — City Attorney

Chief Administrative Officer

Departments and Boards Appointed by Mayor with Council Approval

Fire
Police
Library
Parks
Planning
Public Works
Airport
Personnel
Harbor
Water and Power
etc.

(1) Elected at-large from 1916-80, by districts before and after that. The mayor sits and votes as a council member.

(2) Elected at-large except 1977-80.

(3) Mayor and council separate; Mayor has veto power, appoints department heads and advisory commissions.

(4) Elected by district.

(5) Mayor and Council separate; Mayor has veto power.

Source: From POLITICS IN THE GOLDEN STATE by Terry Christiansen and Larry N. Gerston. Copyright © 1984 by Terry Christiansen and Larry N. Gerston. Scott, Foresman and Company.

The *council-manager* type of government gives the city council both executive and legislative power, but the council exercises its executive power by appointing a professionally trained city manager to coordinate and administer city departments. In this form of government, the mayor has largely ceremonial responsibilities and is usually chosen by the council from among its own members, rather than by the voters. A number of city governments contain some characteristics of both the mayor-council and the council-manager types.

Los Angeles, San Francisco, and San Bernardino employ the mayor-council form, while San Diego, Oakland, San Jose, and Torrance are among the two thirds of all cities in the state that have adopted the newer council-manager form. Under either system, most cities have a city clerk, attorney, treasurer, and planning commission. The most common departments are police, fire, public works, recreation and parks, and building. A resident with a complaint about city services had best do his or her homework regarding the structure of city government in order to get fastest and most helpful response. If the bureaucracy that controls the street cleaning services is not responsive, the resident with a dirty street must understand which of the elected officials is most directly responsible for that section of the city in order to obtain some street-cleaning. City employees, while generally hardworking and concerned, may go the extra mile if the staff of a city council member makes a special request for a constituent.

City Politics

The forces that influence city politics are even more varied than the forms of city government. Homeowners, builders, unions, historic preservationists, environmentalists, realtors, and renters are among the groups that vie for clout in the city's decision-making process. As in most political campaigns, incumbents tend to have the advantage, but an incumbent who has made enough enemies can be ousted by a well-organized newcomer.

One of the factors in city politics that is in the process of major change is the way in which council members are elected. In most of California's 450 cities, council members are elected *at-large*, that is, they may live anywhere in the city. Only a few cities use *district* elections that divide the city into geographic areas from which council members are elected. For years, the argument for at-large elections was that the most qualified people could get into office regardless of their address. However, this often meant that whole sections of cities, particularly those inhabited by ethnic minorities, were not represented on the council due to the financial advantages of the whites from more affluent areas who ran for office. In 1988, a federal appeals court ruled that residents in any city with at-large elections who believe that the current system undermines the political power of the city's ethnic minorities may challenge the at-large system and demand district elections. The ruling, based on a case brought by the Mexican American Legal Defense and Education Fund on behalf of the Latino population of Watsonville in Santa Cruz County, required that electoral districts be created so that Latinos, who make up nearly 50 percent of the city's population, could gain some seats on the council.[1] This ruling could be the beginning of a shift from at-large to district elections in cities throughout the state, and could ultimately lead to far more minority representation on city councils, as well as the opportunity for other less-well-financed candidates to get into office.

The battle for power that goes on between elections is most likely to be waged at city council meetings, council committee hearings, or commission hearings. At these, residents affected by a potential ordinance are empowered to speak to the issues before the decision-making body. The Brown Act of 1953 guarantees that all local government meetings be open to the public except when personnel matters, legal actions, labor negotiations, or property deals are being discussed. Public notice of meetings and their agendas must be made available in advance, although these notices are often tucked away in little-read newspapers, and few city residents can keep track of all the decisions that affect their daily lives.

As in all levels of government, city policies are often determined by those who are most able to contribute to campaigns. It is at the city level, however, that other well-organized groups can get involved successfully. The nearly fifty neighborhood homeowner groups that belong to the Federation of Hillside and Canyon Associations of Los Angeles coalesced successfully with other grassroots organizations to help pass the city's slow-growth Proposition U in 1986, despite opposition from a well-financed group of developers and builders. Rent control laws, environmental protections, and comparable worth pay systems for city employees are the types of issues that well-organized voters can control at the local level.

City Finances

Until 1978, cities obtained about one-fourth of their revenues from local property taxes. After Proposition 13 slashed this source, cities both cut back many services and turned to Sacramento for assistance.

Utility taxes and sales taxes help cities fill out their budgets, while many cities have increased the fees charged for building permits, recreational facilities, garbage collection, and other services. Business licenses, traffic fines, and some federal support are additional sources of revenue. Despite their relatively diverse funding sources, few cities enjoy the luxury of being able to spend freely, and most city governments spend a great deal of time deciding how best to allocate the scarce resources available. Police departments usually obtain the largest chunk of city monies, leaving fire services, streets, parks and other departments to battle for their share of the pie.

Reference Note

1. *Los Angeles Times*, July 28, 1988, Part I, p. 1.

13

Counties, Special Districts, and Regional Agencies

Of all governing bodies, local governments are closest to the people and affect them most personally through such services as crime prevention, traffic regulation, and the operation of public schools. One might hope, therefore, that they would be the easiest to understand and control. Because of the large numbers of local governments and their confusing and overlapping jurisdictions, however, this is not the case.

Counties

California's fifty-eight counties run the gamut in both geographic size and population. Los Angeles County, with eight million residents, is the most populated in the nation. San Bernardino County, with its 20,000 square miles, is the largest; recent efforts to break San Bernardino into two counties were defeated at the ballot box. In contrast, Alpine County, which borders Nevada near Lake Tahoe, has about 1500 residents, and San Francisco, the only combined city-county in the state, comprises only 49 square miles (see Figure 13.1).

In addition to providing the basic services of police, fire protection, libraries, parks, and recreation to inhabitants of unincorporated areas, the counties also provide another complete set of services to all residents, both those in cities and those in unincorporated areas.

These programs include administration of assistance programs such as Aid to Families with Dependent Children (AFDC); the maintenance of property ownership, birth, and marriage records; the prosecution of major crimes; the provision of health services (including mental health) to the indigent; and control of public health problems such as highly contagious diseases, outbreaks of food poisoning, etc.

In order to adequately provide these varied services, counties must receive substantial financial support from the state and federal governments. The nationwide assistance programs such as AFDC receive most of their monies from the federal government, while the state provides a large measure of funding for the county's health care programs and the public protection agencies such as courts, district attorney, and county jail. Like the cities, counties were more financially independent of Sacramento before Proposition 13 (1978). Since then, counties have had to depend heavily on the state to make up for lost property tax revenues (see Figure 13.2).

It is for this reason that one of the most difficult issues facing counties today is the annual funding crisis generated when county appropriations are cut by state decisions. In 1988, Los Angeles County's entire mental health program was nearly destroyed by a gubernatorial veto, leaving seriously disturbed people without care.[1] Only by cutting other programs could the county have found the funds for mental health—a program whose primary constituents are often in no position to lobby for themselves.

Another issue involves the jurisdictional problems of cities and counties, which often provide identical services in virtually the same community. County sheriff's departments continue to serve residents of unincorporated areas just blocks from where those same services are provided by city police departments. Despite periodic waves of reform sentiment, no unit of government has been willing to disband or reduce its forces in order to eliminate the overlap.

A final problem for counties is the issue of adequate representation. With the exception of San Francisco, with its combined city-county status and eleven-member Boards of Supervisors, all counties are governed by five-member Boards of Supervisors, exercising both legislative and executive powers. In less populated counties, five individuals may be sufficient; in counties such as Los Angeles, the idea of five members serving eight million residents has often been criticized as inadequate. A recent federal court ruling has added a new factor to the concerns about Los Angeles County's representation: It held that the county, like the city of Los Angeles (see

Figure 13.1 The counties of California, 1984

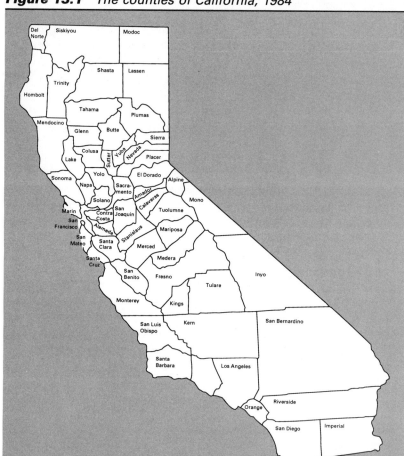

Figure 13.2 *The Los Angeles County Budget*

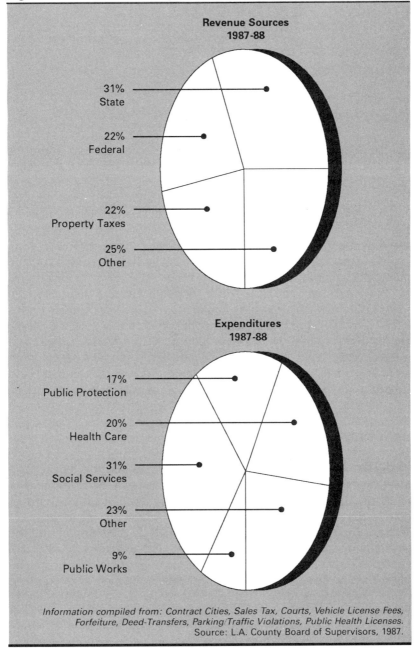

Revenue Sources
1987-88

31%
State

22%
Federal

22%
Property Taxes

25%
Other

Expenditures
1987-88

17%
Public Protection

20%
Health Care

31%
Social Services

23%
Other

9%
Public Works

Information compiled from: Contract Cities, Sales Tax, Courts, Vehicle License Fees, Forfeiture, Deed-Transfers, Parking/Traffic Violations, Public Health Licenses.
Source: L.A. County Board of Supervisors, 1987.

Chapter 4) must realign its five supervisorial districts in order to lower barriers to the election of Latinos. Many observers believe that the court's ruling will eventually lead to the creation of a larger Board of Supervisors that could allow for greater representation from the various ethnic groups in the county, some of whom, like blacks and Latinos, have never had a member of their group elected to the Board.

Special Districts

Special districts are created when a service is needed that cannot be provided by the city or county. The vast majority of California's special districts are school districts. Other types include those providing water, street lighting, mosquito abatement, transportation, and air pollution control. Normally, each district performs only one task. School districts have their own elected governing boards, while the remaining special districts are governed either by the county board of supervisors or by specially chosen bodies often appointed by mayors or other local officials.

Special districts range in size from small cemetery districts to the Metropolitan Water District of Southern California, which serves eight counties and wields enormous political clout. Other large special districts are the Southern California Rapid Transit District and the Bay Area Rapid Transit District. The many special districts, both large and small, add to the fragmentation of local government and subsequent confusion of citizens who utilize their various services.

School Districts

Of all the services provided by local governments, the biggest and most expensive is public education. This service is the responsibility of more than eleven hundred special districts, including approximately 700 elementary school districts, 115 high school districts, 71 community college districts, and 265 unified districts providing both elementary and high school programs. These districts each have elected boards whose members are directly accountable to the voters. Their chief revenue source is the state, with some monies still derived from local property taxes. California's schools, once among the best in the nation, have slipped to embarrassingly low rankings in such measures as per-pupil expenditures, in which the state ranked 26th in 1987, and the percentage of personal income spent on public education.[2] Ironically enough, the higher education system, which includes the University of California and the California State University campuses, gives California an international image as a place in which to get an outstanding college education. In between the K-12 and the university systems are the 107 community colleges, which enable over 1.2 million Californians to earn credits for university transfer or receive vocational training.

Regional Agencies

The purpose of regional agencies is to coordinate the tasks and plans of all the various local government units in a region. Two of the most important regional agencies are the Association of Bay Area Governments, representing nine counties and 92 cities in the San Francisco area, and the Southern California Association of Governments, including representatives from six counties and 130 cities. These associations coordinate policies on everything from air and water pollution to housing and growth decisions. Unfortunately, perhaps, the regional agencies are only advisory in nature; their recommendations are not binding on any of the cities or counties that compose their membership.

Despite their current lack of power, regional agencies or their equivalents may eventually gain more political force. The Los Angeles 2000 Committee, a group of 150 business and community leaders that spent over two years studying the city's problems, has suggested that a new "super-agency" be formed to both make policy and implement it.[3] One possible prototype of this kind of regional super-agency is the Southern California Air Quality Management District (SCAQMD) whose 1988 Air Quality Management Plan has the authority to insist that cities within SCAQMD's jurisdiction implement policies that reduce air pollution. This sort of regional effort, which results in the weakening of the powers of locally elected officials, will probably be used more frequently as issues of pollution, transportation and housing become unsolvable at the municipal level.

Reference Notes

1. *Los Angeles Times*, August 1, 1988, Part I, p. 3 and 15.
2. Terry Christensen and Larry N. Gerston, *Politics in the Golden State*, 2nd ed., Scott, Foresman/Little, Brown, 1988, p. 202.
3. *Los Angeles Times*, November 16, 1988, Part I, p. 1.

14

Financing the Golden State

For fiscal years 1988 and 1989, under Republican Governor George Deukmejian, California had the largest state budget of any in the nation—$39 billion for 1988 and $42 billion for 1989. Some might take these huge numbers as an excuse for labeling the Governor with those politically deadly words "big spender." However, given the range of services required to meet the needs of the state's growing population, many Californians (including some legislators), believed that the budgets were inadequate. In either case, there are only a few choices for government: provide less service as a way to keep taxes down, or continue services by raising taxes or borrowing. Even to maintain current levels of government services requires increasing revenues because the costs of salaries, utilities, paper, and all the other requisites of government continue to rise. And government is rarely asked to merely continue current services—rather it is always barraged with demands to expand services and add new ones.

How can it all be accomplished? Californians, like many Americans, want to have their cake and eat it, too.

How the Budget is Developed

Every January, the Governor must present to the legislature a budget plan reflecting the Governor's priorities. This budget requires many months of preparation and input from the executive branch's various departments and agencies. The legislature has about six weeks to respond with its version of an appropriate budget. During those weeks, the Legislative Analyst's office reviews the governor's expenditure requests and revenue projections and provides each legislator with comments. Then the legislature begins public hearings by various subcommittees. During these hearings, members of the public, often represented by lobbyists, as well as many government employees at all levels explain why their particular *appropriations* must be retained or perhaps expanded (see Figure 14.1).

In May, the governor submits his "revision" budget, which takes into account changes in state revenues and other pertinent data. Soon after, the legislature is supposed to send a final version of the budget to the governor. If the Assembly and Senate disagree on specific items, a conference committee must be formed to work out the differences. The state constitution requires that the legislature complete their work on the budget and send it to the governor by June 15. Due to the differing priorities within the legislature, however, the struggle over budget choices often drags on through July.

When the governor receives the legislature's budget bill, he can then utilize the *item veto* to reduce appropriations or even eliminate whole programs. The legislature rarely has the votes to override such item vetoes, leaving the Governor in ultimate control over the state budget.

Sources of Revenue

The five major sources of money for the state are:

1. the general fund, which includes state income tax, sales taxes, bank and corporations taxes, and interest earned by the state on money not currently in use;
2. special funds, earmarked for particular programs, including motor vehicle license and registration fees, gasoline taxes, and portions of the sales, cigarette, and horse racing taxes;
3. bond funds, which are monies borrowed from investors for specific purposes and returned to them with interest in the future—voters must approve all state borrowing by majority votes;
4. federal funds, including "free" money and some monies that require matching state or local commitments;
5. miscellaneous revenues, such as college housing fees, contributions to state pension plans, etc. (see figure 14.2)

Figure 14.1 California state budget process

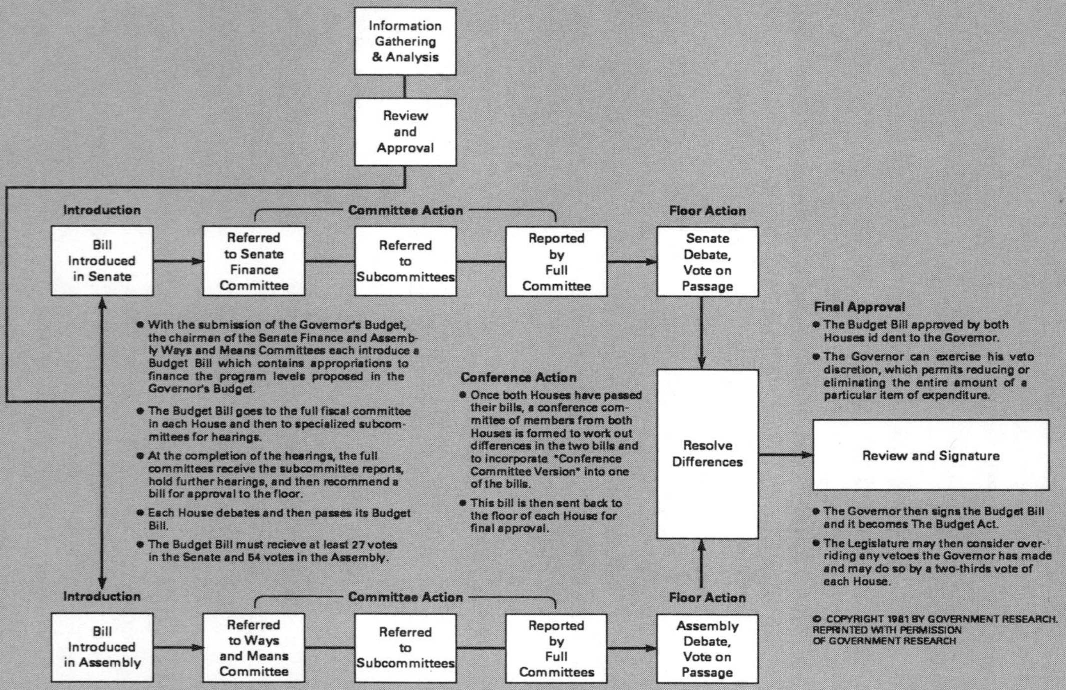

Introduction

Bill Introduced in Senate

Committee Action

Referred to Senate Finance Committee

Referred to Subcommittees

Reported by Full Committee

Information Gathering & Analysis

Review and Approval

Floor Action

Senate Debate, Vote on Passage

Resolve Differences

Final Approval

• The Budget Bill approved by both Houses is sent to the Governor.

• The Governor can exercise his veto discretion, which permits reducing or eliminating the entire amount of a particular item of expenditure.

Review and Signature

• The Governor then signs the Budget Bill and it becomes The Budget Act.

• The Legislature may then consider overriding any vetoes the Governor has made and may do so by a two-thirds vote of each House.

• With the submission of the Governor's Budget, the chairmen of the Senate Finance and Assembly Ways and Means Committees each introduce a Budget Bill which contains appropriations to finance the program levels proposed in the Governor's Budget.

• The Budget Bill goes to the full fiscal committee in each House and then to specialized subcommittees for hearings.

• At the completion of the hearings, the full committees receive the subcommittee reports, hold further hearings, and then recommend a bill for approval on the floor.

• Each House debates and then passes its Budget Bill.

• The Budget Bill must receive at least 27 votes in the Senate and 54 votes in the Assembly.

Conference Action

• Once both Houses have passed their bills, a conference committee of members from both Houses is formed to work out differences in the two bills and to incorporate a "Conference Committee Version" into one of the bills.

• This bill is then sent back to the floor of each House for final approval.

Introduction

Bill Introduced in Assembly

Committee Action

Referred to Ways and Means Committee

Referred to Subcommittees

Reported by Full Committees

Floor Action

Assembly Debate, Vote on Passage

• COPYRIGHT 1981 BY GOVERNMENT RESEARCH. REPRINTED WITH PERMISSION OF GOVERNMENT RESEARCH

Source: California Department of Finance.

Figure 14.2 *Revenues and expenditures, 1988–89 fiscal year*

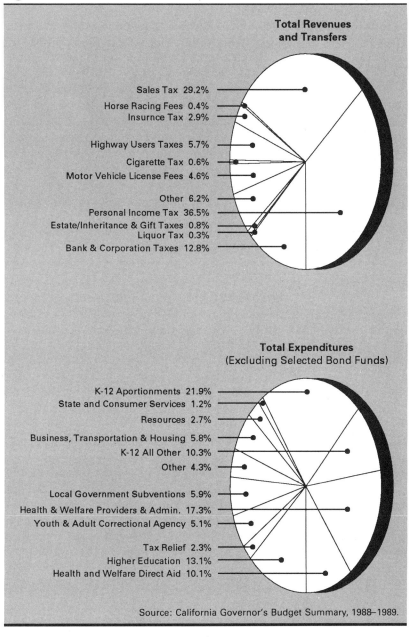

Total Revenues and Transfers

Sales Tax 29.2%
Horse Racing Fees 0.4%
Insurnce Tax 2.9%

Highway Users Taxes 5.7%

Cigarette Tax 0.6%
Motor Vehicle License Fees 4.6%

Other 6.2%
Personal Income Tax 36.5%
Estate/Inheritance & Gift Taxes 0.8%
Liquor Tax 0.3%
Bank & Corporation Taxes 12.8%

Total Expenditures (Excluding Selected Bond Funds)

K-12 Aportionments 21.9%
State and Consumer Services 1.2%
Resources 2.7%
Business, Transportation & Housing 5.8%
K-12 All Other 10.3%
Other 4.3%

Local Government Subventions 5.9%
Health & Welfare Providers & Admin. 17.3%
Youth & Adult Correctional Agency 5.1%

Tax Relief 2.3%
Higher Education 13.1%
Health and Welfare Direct Aid 10.1%

Source: California Governor's Budget Summary, 1988–1989.

Controversies over these revenue sources are endless. Which ones should be raised? Which lowered? Business interests want to reduce corporate taxes as well as to repeal the "unitary tax" that taxes California's multinational corporations based on their worldwide profits rather than simply on profits earned within the state. Voters seem to go through phases in terms of their acceptance of state borrowing, with the recent trends indicating support for *bond issues*, which finance such projects as cleaning up drinking water and toxic wastes, financing low-interest home loans for veterans, building prisons, constructing schools, and creating parks and open space. Other groups interested in tax policies include grassroots lobbies such as the Citizens for Tax Justice and special interests such as the highway, liquor, and horse racing lobbies.

Voter Decisions and State Finance

In addition to voting on bond measures, voters often have input into fiscal policy through ballot initiatives. One of the turning points for California's tax policies was Proposition 13 of June 1978, also known as the Jarvis-Gann initiative, in recognition of the efforts of landlord Howard Jarvis and his ally Paul Gann to get the initiative on the ballot.

The roots of Proposition 13 lie in the massive national and international inflation of the early 1970s. While the causes of the inflationary spiral were primarily outside California, including such factors as heavy federal spending in the 1960s and the oil embargo of the early 1970s, these circumstances, added to the traditional speculation in land and property in the state, fueled an enormous rise in the real estate values on which property taxes are levied. People who had lived in homes for years were suddenly confronted with doubled and tripled tax assessments from their county assessor. Faced with the risk of losing their homes, middle and low-income homeowners gladly joined Jarvis and other major property holders in supporting Proposition 13. When public employees claimed that the proposition would not only cut property taxes but also cut public services, Jarvis replied that "only the fat" would be cut and that the state budget would rescue counties, cities, and school districts if necessary.

These arguments were extremely persuasive—Proposition 13 passed by a landslide. Since a budget surplus had accumulated in Sacramento, the state did "bail out" the local governments for a while, but many services were cut back, including library accessability, fine arts and athletics in the schools, and parks and recreation. Additionally, Proposition 13 had some unforeseen longterm impacts, including the shift from local control to a Sacramento-based funding system for most of the cities, counties, and special districts. Other flaws in the measure include the fact that property owners who rarely sell (such as commercial property owners) have almost no increase in taxes whereas owners of individual homes, which are sold more frequently, confront reassessments up to the current market value, causing dramatic tax increases.

Many observers believe that the reductions in local property taxes caused by Proposition 13 and the subsequent shift to state-controlled funding of local government has contributed to the crisis in services experienced in many areas today. In Butte County, for example, officials have seriously considered the option of disbanding county government due to lack of funds. School districts and cities, along with counties, must go on annual "begging" expeditions to Sacramento, and, if the state has a year of low revenues, the amounts allotted to the local governments can be reduced dramatically.

Another important fiscal measure of the 1970s (the era of the so-called "taxpayers' revolt") was Proposition 4 of 1979. Also known as the Gann initiative, after Paul Gann, this proposition placed a cap on public expenditures once a specified limit was reached. Prior to Proposition 4, the state's only limitation was the amount of revenue it collected. Under Gann's initiative, expenditure increases are limited to the rates of inflation and population growth. After that amount is used, no further tax monies can be spent. In 1987 the cap was reached for the first time, causing Governor Deukmejian to call for a tax rebate of the "excess" monies in the state treasury. Based on budget predictions, the state returned to taxpayers approximately $1.1 billion in the fall of that year with the average taxpayer receiving about $64. To the embarrassment of many in his party, only a few months later the Governor had to admit to an "error" in predictions that had left the state *not* with a surplus but rather with a $1 billion shortfall in revenues. To deal with the shortfall, the Governor initially proposed a tax increase which he called "temporary minimal adjustments." However, even the Republicans in the legislature refused to join him in making these adjustments and the state budget was adopted without the usual reserve and with substantial cuts in programs.

Efforts to undo the Gann limit, such as Proposition 71 (defeated in June 1988), have yet to "uncap" the state and permit government to spend what it collects. School enrollments, along with prison and pollution control costs, are rising faster than either inflation or total population growth; meanwhile, voters continue their efforts to get government to provide needed services without raising their property, income, or sales taxes. Such efforts include Proposition 37 (1984), which created the state-run lottery that divides its revenues into administrative costs, prizes, and education, and Proposition 99 (November 1988), which increased cigarette taxes to provide funds for medical research and medical care for those with tobacco-related diseases. Also passed in November 1988 was the controversial Proposition 98, the school-funding initiative, calling for approximately one-third of the state's annual budget to be devoted to K-12 and community college education. While spending for schools appears noncontroversial, many who opposed the initiative believe that its implementation will require massive cuts in noneducational items in the state budget.

Future Prospects

The sources of government funds depend, ultimately, on the vitality of the state's economy. California has generally been a growing and economically vibrant region with its "high-tech" industries, agriculture, military contracts, oil, entertainment, and tourist industries. Future economic links with Asia also bode well for the state's well-being. Nevertheless, dissatisfaction with growth and the pollution, traffic congestion, school overcrowding, and other blights that accompany it has already created the new voter revolt of our times: the slow-growth movement. This important trend, as well as other issues facing California in the last decade of the century, form the basis of the next and final chapter.

15

Issues for the 1990s

Although life in the Golden State is supposed to be sunny and sweet, Californians are increasingly discovering that the difficulties of daily life are accompanied by constant stress. For many, their encounters with air pollution, unhealthful beaches, overcrowded schools, dirty streets, or horrendous traffic congestion have motivated them to become active in efforts to improve the quality of life. Thus, daily frustrations have become the stuff of which political movements are made. Even in smaller communities that were once exempt from such problems, many Californians feel the encroachment of the same difficulties they had hoped to avoid when they chose to live there.

Each of these issues has its own set of causes and, hopefully, its own set of solutions. Some links do exist, however. One common theme has recently become the primary grassroots focal point of the 1990s: *slow-growth*. Like the tax revolt of the 70s, the slow-growth movement is coalescing throughout the state, in both large cities and small towns. The issues it addresses and the people to whom it appeals are numerous and diverse. Everything from water shortages to crime and inadequate mass transit can be blamed on the high growth rates of the state, and those who are banding together to try to slow the pace include everyone from left-leaning Democrats to conservative Republicans.

Roots of the Slow-Growth Movement

The first signs of an incipient movement to oppose growth occurred in Bay Area cities such as Livermore, Pleasanton, and Alameda in the early 1970s, when voters passed measures that imposed *moratoriums* on building permits and prevented construction of multi-family units. By the end of the decade, particularly after the service reductions caused by Proposition 13, voters in such diverse southern locations as Santa Barbara, Redlands, Riverside, and Thousand Oaks had also learned to utilize local initiatives to gain similar growth controls (see Figure 15.1).

The passage of these initiatives stemmed from a clear appeal to peoples' basic needs: the need for safe and uncongested neighborhoods; the need for adequate schools, police, and fire services; the need for open space, clean air, and water. All of these needs appeared to be threatened by: 1) the continuing issuance of building permits, 2) the increased density created by construction of multi-unit buildings where single-family homes once stood, and 3) the destruction of agricultural lands for new housing tracts and commercial developments.

Isolated organizations composed of environmentalists, historic preservationists, homeowners, and even horse owners, came to realize that their interests were not separate concerns but rather mutual ones. By the end of the 1980s what had begun as a collection of local movements had coalesced into several regional organizations that appeared to be heading for a statewide umbrella coalition under the general theme of "planned growth" advocacy.

The "Pro-Growth" Backlash

Like all social movements, the planned growth movement has a countervailing force with which to reckon. As each local or regional initiative is proposed, those who favor growth fight tooth and nail to protect their rights to continue building and developing. This opposition includes the California Association of Realtors, the Building Industry Association, and many politicians and economists who support the "free-market" approach to growth issues. Their arguments range from the ideological: "let market forces determine what is built and where," to the practical: "if we stop or slow building, the law of supply and demand will force housing costs up" (see Figure 15.2). Their allies are frequently unions whose members work in construction or related trades, those who fear that growth limitations will increase unemployment, and small land owners and developers wanting to build in order to maximize their financial gains.

Much to the chagrin of those who support planned growth, some of the practical objections raised by the "free growth" advocates have proven valid. Housing costs have risen at astronomical rates in the

Figure 15.1 *Geographical distribution of successful growth control initiatives (1972–1988)*

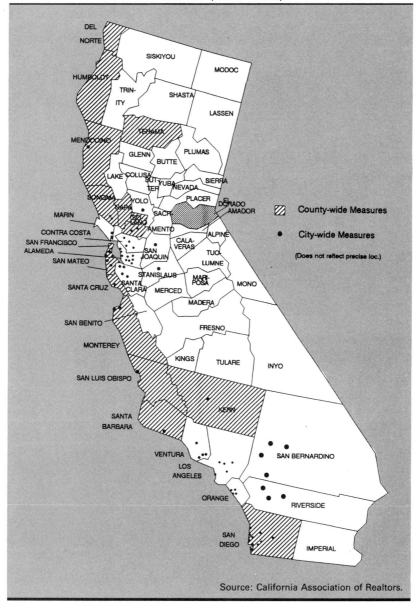

Source: California Association of Realtors.

Figure 15.2 *Median sales price of existing homes*

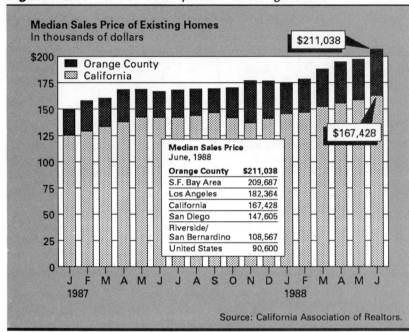

Median Sales Price of Existing Homes
In thousands of dollars

$211,038

■ Orange County
▧ California

$167,428

Median Sales Price June, 1988	
Orange County	**$211,038**
S.F. Bay Area	209,687
Los Angeles	182,364
California	167,428
San Diego	147,605
Riverside/ San Bernardino	108,567
United States	90,600

J F M A M J J A S O N D | J F M A M J
1987 | 1988

Source: California Association of Realtors.

state, with the median price of existing homes ranging from $108,000 in the San Bernardino/Riverside area to $211,000 in Orange County (see chart). A Los Angeles Times-Orange County Poll in June, 1988 indicated that a whopping 84 percent of all Orange County residents believed that "children growing up in Orange County will not be able to afford housing here as adults."[1]

Nevertheless, despite fears about housing costs, polls also indicate that 50 percent of Californians favor a temporary moratorium on all economic development or a slowdown of economic growth,[2] both of which present a direct challenge to the pro-growth ethos of American capitalism and California's own history of rapid development. While the pro-growth advocates tend to have large amounts of money for campaigns, the planned growth organizations are increasing in number and are even considering running a slow-growth candidate for governor in 1990.[3] Perhaps one hopeful sign for an eventual compromise between the two sides was the UCLA School of Public Policy's 1988 forum on the "Growth Controversy," an event that drew over 500 slow-growth and pro-growth advocates from throughout the state into dialogue with each other. Unless more discussion occurs between the planned growth movement and its opposition, Californians can look forward only to more ballot initiatives, city council battles, and other political struggles over the state's future.

Other Issues and Portents

Although almost every major policy issue in the state may ultimately be related to the growth issue, there are numerous other matters to which Californians are directing their attention. Despite the daunting nature of some of them, reasons for hope emerge as both politicians and grassroots activists join together to find solutions to the state's problems. Assimilating new immigrants, reducing overcrowding in schools, diminishing gang and drug-related violence, improving transportation corridors, and providing adequate water supplies for both crops and urban dwellers are among the many issues attracting attention.

In response to the rapid increase of foreign-born immigrants to the state, several school districts have opened special centers for immigrant students in order to facilitate a more rapid transition into the routine of the American school system. These centers provide students and their families with videos, bilingual staff members, cultural information, and shortcuts through the red tape of entering school.[4] With this more structured assistance, the transition for both school-age children and their families may be easier as they learn the rules of life in California, from immunization requirements to acceptable forms of discipline.

Another potential improvement in schools is the growing use of year-round scheduling that makes facilities available for a full twelve months instead of the traditional nine-month calendar. For districts such as Long Beach and Los Angeles, the school age population has simply outgrown the number of schools. Even with the recent approval of state bonds for school construction, finding enough available land in the dense inner cities can be almost impossible. In some cases, housing must be destroyed in order to build schools, although the policy of most school boards is to minimize the demolition of housing when seeking construction sites. Even as new schools are built, overcrowding and "busing-out" continue in some districts, with the bused children being primarily low-income, minority youths transported to underutilized schools in the suburbs. Although middle-class parents whose children have not been in overcrowded classrooms frequently protest the change, year-round schools may be the only way in which densely populated districts can educate all their pupils.

Even as efforts continue to assist the educational system, other institutions also are called upon to help solve California's problems. Gang violence, while hardly under control, is being confronted by everything from prayer meetings and "truces" to civil lawsuits. In the Highland Park area of Los Angeles, a crime-ridden apartment complex was transformed when the owner was threatened with a lawsuit for violating the Controlled Substances Abatement Act, a 1971 law that allows the city attorney or any private person to sue the owner of a property that is being consistently used for "selling, storing, giving away or manufacturing controlled substances".[5] Under the provisions of the act, the owner could be held liable for permitting such activities on his or her property. When the Highland Park owner cleaned up the gang graffiti, installed lights and fences, and hired security guards, the residents experienced not only a decrease in drug dealing but also in burglaries and assaults. While not all property owners comply so easily, the threat of a civil suit may become a new crime-fighting tactic in other cities as well. In a different and less direct effort to curb gang violence and rechannel the energies of inner city youth, the Urban Impact Program of the Los Angeles Department of Recreation and Parks has allocated substantial funds to inner city parks in order to narrow the gap between those facilities and the recreational services available to higher-income suburban residents.[6]

One of the problems that affects the wealthy nearly as much as the poor is the condition of transportation in the state. While the poor may have to depend on public transportation to a greater degree, even the wealthiest Californian cannot escape the horrendous traffic of virtually every urban area. During the Deukmejian era, emphasis has been placed on highway construction and improvements rather than on public mass transit. Although Californians, particularly the southern variety, are known for their "love affair" with their cars, eventually they may have to accept the shared spaces of public mass transit in order to be able to move from one place to another. In the short-run, concepts such as the double-decking of certain sections of very congested freeways may be utilized to ease the predicted *gridlock* of the 1990s. Eventually, however, it may be impossible to provide enough highways or even double-decked freeways for the numbers of private cars that are expected on the roads. In addition to fixed-rail systems such as BART in the Bay Area, the San Diego trolley, and the Sacramento Rapid Transit Metro, other innovations to solve gridlock include more systematic and regulated carpooling by employees in large businesses, staggered work schedules to avoid rush hour standstills, and ultimately, the restructuring of housing patterns to enable people to live near their work.

Like the issue of how to transport people from one place to another, the question of how to provide adequate water supplies to Californians is one of the oldest and most difficult in the state. Geography itself sets the stage for this century-old conflict: the north has 66 percent of the state's rain and snow and the south, including the agricultural belt, uses 80 percent of the resulting water.[7] While environmentalists are concerned about such problems as the drying up of Mono Lake and the depletion of striped bass and salmon in the Central Valley streams, farm interests insist on their share of the water for one of California's most important industries, and urban dwellers worry about rising costs and recurrent shortages. Court decisions delineating the standards for water allocation interact with the decisions of the Water Resources Control Board in an attempt to balance the competing needs in the state. While no fresh ideas or brilliant solutions are on the horizon, the movers and shakers of California politics are focusing attention on this issue as the growing population brings insistent demands for a reasonable solution.

Although the list of California's problems and her peoples' attempts to solve them could go on endlessly, the ultimate issue for the future is how much effort the residents of the Golden State will be willing to invest in their own future. Will Californians continue to cajole and pressure their political leaders to define the issues, formulate possible solutions, and make tough choices? Or will they abdicate their personal responsibility and let the "powers that be" make decisions for them? With the state's long history of strong democratic institutions and pioneer-spirited citizens, the portents for the future are bright. Californians have risen to many challenges before; why should the 1990s be any different?

Reference Notes

1. *Los Angeles Times,* Orange County Edition, August 7, 1988, Part I, p. 3.
2. *Los Angeles Times,* August 2, 1988, Part I, p. 15.
3. *Los Angeles Times,* December 12, 1988, Part I, p. 3.
4. *Los Angeles Independent,* July 2, 1988, p. 1.
5. *Los Angeles Times,* August 4, 1988, Glendale Section, p. 1.
6. *Los Angeles Independent,* July 28, 1988, p. 1.
7. Michael J. Ross, *California: Its Government and Politics,* 3rd ed., Brooks/Cole, 1988, p. 22.

Bibliography

Baus, Herbert M., and William B. Ross, *Politics Battle Plan* (N.Y.: Macmillian, 1968).

Book of the States 1988-89 (Lexington, KY: Council of State Governments, 1988).

California Blue Book (Sacramento: State Printing Office, 1979).

Constitution of the U.S. and Constitution of the State of California 1985-86 (Sacramento: California State Senate, 1985).

Culver, John H., and John C. Syer, *Power and Politics in California* (N.Y.: John Wiley & Sons, 1980).

Delmatier, Royce D., Clarence F. McIntosh, and Earl G. Waters, eds., *The Rumble of California Politics* (N.Y.: John Wiley & Sons, Inc., 1970).

Driscoll, James D., *California Legislature,* Revised Ed. (Sacramento: Center for Research and Education in Government, 1987).

Elder, Ann H. and George C. Kiser, *Governing American States and Communities* (Glenview, IL: Scott, Foresman and Company, 1983).

Harvey, Richard B., *The Dynamics of California Government and Politics,* 2nd ed. (Monterey: Brooks/Cole, 1985).

Hoeber, et al, Thomas R., and Charles M. Price, eds., *California Government and Politics Annual 1987-88* (Sacramento: California Center for Research and Education in Government, 1987).

Kotkin, Joel, and Paul Grabowicz, *California, Inc.* (New York: Avon Books, 1982).

Lee, Eugene C., and Larry L. Berg, ed., *The Challenge of California,* 2nd ed. (Boston: Little, Brown and Company, 1976).

Municipal Yearbook, 1988 (Washington, D.C.: International City Management Association, 1988).

Quinn, T. Anthony, and Ed Salzman, *California Public Administration* (Sacramento: California Journal Press, 1982).

Rolle, Andrew F., *California,* 2nd ed. (N.Y.: Thomas Y. Crowell Company, 1969).

Samish, Arthur H., with Richard Thomas, *The Secret Boss of California* (N.Y.: Crown Publishers, 1971).

Starr, Kevin, *Inventing the Dream* (N.Y.: Oxford University Press, 1985).

Glossary

AFDC Aid to Families with Dependent Children. Established by the 1935 Social Security Act, the most controversial and costly "welfare" program.

Appropriations Laws allocating specific amounts of money for designated governmental purposes, or the amounts of money themselves.

At-large In contrast to district elections, a method of electing members of a city council or other legislative body by voters of the entire governmental unit.

Bail A refundable amount of money deposited in behalf of a criminal defendant in return for which he or she is released from jail until the time of the trial.

Bicameral A legislative body consisting of two parts, or "houses," such as the California Legislature, consisting of the Senate and Assembly.

Block grants Financial assistance from the national government to the states, or from the state to local governments, for use in broadly designated areas such as health or job training.

Boards of Supervisors County governing bodies passing laws, often known as ordinances, and exercising executive power as well by "supervising" most of the departments that administer them.

Bond issues Interest-bearing government securities, authorized at the state or local level by voter approval of a ballot proposition, by which money is borrowed for prison construction or some other purpose not involving current operating expenses.

Budget A proposed annual spending plan through which a chief executive requests the legislature to appropriate a specific amount of money for each government program and designates revenue sources to defray the costs.

Civil liberties Protected types of behavior such as freedom of speech or religion, which governments are prohibited from taking away.

Civil rights Legally imposed obligations, such as the right to equal protection of the laws or reasonable bail, that governments owe to individuals.

Civil service system A set of procedures for hiring government employees on the basis of merit, usually demonstrated by examination, and protecting them against unjust firing.

Closed primary The kind of primary used in California and most other states in which only voters registered as members of a political party can vote for the nomination (selection) of that party's candidates.

Compromise of 1850 A group of laws introduced by Sen. Henry Clay of Kentucky, which settled the slavery dispute for about 10 years and included California's admission as a free state (one in which slavery was prohibited.)

Conference committee A temporary committee appointed to resolve differences between the senate and assembly versions of a bill if one house adds an amendment which the other house rejects.

Constitutional officers The executive officials that the state constitution requires be elected by the voters.

Council-manager A form of city government in which the elected city council, with legislative authority, appoints, and can fire, a city manager to whom the public works and other executive departments are responsible.

District A portion of a governmental unit from which a single legislator is elected, often contrasted with a system in which all legislators (city council members, for example) are elected from the entire governmental unit "at-large."

Electoral votes The number of votes a state may cast in electing the President and Vice President, computed by adding the number of its U.S. Senators, two, to the number of its members of the House of Representatives, 45 for California in 1984 and 1988.

Executive clemency The governor's power to lighten criminal sentences imposed by the courts by pardons, which cancel them, commutations, which reduce them, or reprieves, which postpone them; amnesties are pardons for an entire group.

Federal That which refers to a characteristic of federalism, a political system in which, as in the United States, the national and state governments each have some powers independent of the other; sometimes, referring to the national, in contrast to the state, government.

Felonies Major crimes, the trials for which are conducted in superior courts in California, and carrying a possible punishment of a year or more in prison.

Gerrymandered A district whose boundaries have been drawn by a legislature to favor the election of a particular group, individual, or candidate of the dominant political party.

Grants-in-aid Block grants or other types of financial assistance from one level of government to another for more narrowly specified uses, in accordance with prescribed standards and requiring the recipient government to allocate some money for the same uses.

Grassroots Pertaining to actions, movements, or groups of a political nature that rely chiefly on the mass involvement of more or less ordinary citizens.

Gridlock A condition of traffic paralysis in which cars block street intersections; more loosely, heavy, bumper-to-bumper traffic.

Gubernatorial Pertaining to the office of governor.

Indictments Formal accusations of criminal behavior by a grand jury, sometimes used to bring defendants to trial.

Inferior courts In California, the justice, municipal, and superior courts in which trials take place and whose judges are chosen differently than those on the courts of appeal and Supreme Court.

Infractions Violations of the law less serious than most misdemeanors and punishable by no more than small fines.

Initiative The process by which citizens can propose a state or local law or amendment to the state constitution by signing a formal petition asking that it be submitted as a ballot proposition for voter approval.

Issue-oriented organizations Single issue groups interested in public policy on only one issue, such as abortion, or interest groups like the American Civil Liberties Union concerned with a variety of political issues, in contrast with groups primarily concerned with the election of candidates or nonpolitical objectives.

Item veto Sometimes called the line-item veto, the authority of the governor to reduce or eliminate money appropriated by the legislature for a specific purpose while signing the remaining provisions of the bill into law.

K-12 Kindergarten through high school, or the 12th grade.

Lobbying The attempt to influence government policy, usually in behalf of an interest group; a term derived from conversations held in lobbies outside legislative chambers.

Majority More than 50 percent.

Manifest destiny The justification of U.S. territorial expansion based on the mystical assumption that it was the clear, or manifest, fate of the nation to acquire at least all land from the Atlantic to the Pacific Oceans.

Marginal Uncertain, on the edge; a district, in contrast to the more numerous "safe" ones, in which the election outcome is uncertain because neither party has an overwhelming edge in registered voters.

Mayor-council The traditional form of city government based on a separation of powers between a mayor with executive authority and the council with legislative authority, both elected by the voters.

Minimalist That which is limited to its simplest or essential elements; politically, the usually conservative belief that government should do very little.

Minority-majority The demography of an area in which the combined populations of blacks, Latinos, Asians and other racial or ethnic minorities constitute a majority of the area's total population.

Misdemeanors Minor crimes punishable by less than one year in jail.

Moratoriums Delays or interruptions, usually imposed by law, of some usual activity such as loan repayments or the issuance of building permits.

NIMBY Not in My Back Yard. Somewhat sarcastic description of the position of those who want new prisons, garbage dumps, *etc.* as long as they are located in a neighborhood other than their own.

Nonpartisan Elections, such as those of judges, school board members, and city and county officials in California, in which the party affiliation of the candidates may not appear on the ballot.

Office-block ballot To discourage straight party ticket voting, the arrangement of candidates' names according to the office for which they are running rather than their party affiliation.

Override In California, the passage of a law vetoed by the governor, or of that portion item vetoed, by at least a two-thirds vote of the entire Senate and the entire Assembly.

Partisan Elections, such as those of national and most state officials, in which the party affiliation of the candidates appears on the ballot; any action or attitude reflecting strong loyalty to a party or political faction.

Patronage Reward for political suppport in the form of government jobs, contracts, or other benefits.

Plaintiff The person bringing suit in a civil case; along with the defendant or respondent, one of the litigants in the case.

Plea bargaining To reduce the work load of the courts, negotiations in a criminal case designed to get the defendant to plead guilty if the prosecution reduces the seriousness of the charge.

Plurality The most votes, even though it is less than a majority of the total, or the margin of votes by which the winner leads his or her closest opponent.

Political action committee (PAC) An organization, usually formed by an interest group or corporation, designed to solicit money from individuals to be used for campaign contributions to the candidate endorsed by the group.

Political culture The political values, beliefs, and expectations transmitted to most citizens, consciously or unconsciously, by families, schools, churches, the media, and other institutions in a process known as political socialization.

Primaries The elections, held for state and national offices in June of even numbered years in California, to nominate party candidates for the offices to be filled by the general election the following November.

Progressive movement The growing demand in the first dozen years or so of this century for such democratic reforms as the initiative and referendum, and led in California by Hiram Johnson.

Recall A progressive era reform permitting the voters, by petition, to call a special election to remove an official from office before the next regularly scheduled election.

Redistricting Redrawing the boundaries of election districts; required after each census to keep district populations as nearly equal as possible.

Referendums An example of direct, in contrast to representative, democracy in which initiative proposals, bond issues and proposed amendments to the California constitution must be submitted to the voters for approval or rejection.

Restitution Reimbursement or other compensation for damage inflicted, sometimes imposed as an obligation on a convicted criminal to his or her victim by a court or sometimes provided by the state to the victim.

Run-off election In certain nonpartisan races such as those for superior court judge, superintendent of public instruction, or sometimes county supervisor, an election involving the two candidates with the most votes if none of several candidates received a majority in the first election.

Slow-growth The objective of those in the movement to restrict population growth, pollution, or traffic congestion by limiting or imposing a moratorium upon the construction of shopping centers, multi-unit apartments, and so forth.

Speaker The presiding officer and most powerful member of the California Assembly elected to that position by the Assembly from among its own members.

Special districts In contrast to counties and cities that perform many services, local units of government, most commonly school districts, which perform a single function and which often have boundaries different from those of counties and cities.

Standing Committees Permanent committees of the California Senate and Assembly, organized around such policy subjects as education and insurance, to which every bill is referred, and on several of which every legislator serves, and in which most work of the legislature is done.

Statutory-type In contrast to constitutional provisions that normally deal with the structure and procedures of government agencies, provisions normally contained in statutes or laws passed by legislative bodies pertaining to the policies and programs carried out by government agencies.

Third World Pertaining to the predominently poor, largely nonindustrialized or developing nations, mostly in the Southern Hemisphere, or to American blacks, Latinos, and other ethnic groups whose ancestors came from those regions.

Unincorporated areas That territory outside the boundaries of incorporated cities whose residents receive nearly all municipal services from county governments.

Unitary In contrast to a federal system, one in which the county and other regional or local governments have only the powers the state or central government gives to them.

Veto The return of a bill by the president, governor, mayor or other chief executive to the legislature which passed it, unsigned, thereby killing it unless the legislature overrides the veto.

Zoning The legal designation of land, usually by city or county governments, for specified kinds of uses such as residential, commercial, manufacturing, and so forth.

Appendix

Constitutional Officers*

Governor's Office
George Deukmejian (R)
State Capitol
Sacramento 95814
(916) 445-2841
350 McAllister St., #2046
San Francisco 94102
(415) 557-3326
Los Angeles 90005
600 S. Commonwealth Ave., #1200
(213) 736-2373

Cabinet
Michael Frost, Chief of Staff, (916) 445-5106
Jesse Huff, Director of Finance, 445-4141
Shirley Chilton, Sec'y of State and Consumer Services, 445-1935
Gordon Van Vieck, Sec'y of Resources, 445-5656
Jananne Sharpless, Environmental Affairs Advisor, Air Resources Board, 322-5840
Cliff Allenby, Sec'y of Health and Welfare Agency, 445-6951
Jack Parnell, Dir. of Food and Agriculture, 445-7126
Ron Rinaldi, Dir. of Indust. Relations, 324-4163
N. A. Chaderjian, Sec'y of Youth and Adult Correctional Agency, 323-5565
John Geoghegan, Sec'y of Business, Transportation, Housing, 445-1332
David Caffrey, Cabinet Sec'y, 445-8612

*Source: California Department of Finance.

Staff
Michael Frost, Chief of Staff, 445-5106
Richard T. Davis, Special Asst. to Chief of Staff, 324-7988
Allen Zaremberg, Legislative Secretary, 445-0873
Vance Raye, Legal Affairs Sec'y, 445-0873
Greg Kahwajian, Assistant to the Governor, 324-3622
Marvin Baxter, Appointments Sec'y, 445-1915
Susan Pedersen, Scheduling Sec'y, 445-6533
James Robinson, Dir. of Public Affairs and Communication, 445-1682
Huston Cartyle, Local Govt. Affairs Dir., 322-2318
John McCarthy, Community Relations, 445-1114
Kevin Brett, Press Sec'y, 445-4571
Peter G. Mehas, Education Advisor, 323-0611
Sue Sims, Writing and Research Director, 445-1764
Margaret Bengs, Special Asst. for Constitutional Affairs, 445-6343

Lieutenant Governor
Leo McCarthy (D)
Chief of staff: Alan Katz
1028 State Capitol
Sacramento 95814
(916) 445-8994
107 South Broadway, #4007
Los Angeles 90012
(213) 620-2560

Treasurer
Thomas Hayes
915 Capitol Mall, Room 110
Sacramento 95814
(916) 445-5316

Superintend. of Public Instruction
Bill Honig (NP)
  Executive deputy: Dave Dawson
  721 Capitol Mall, Room 24
  Sacramento 95814
  (916) 445-4338

Secretary of State
March Fong Eu (D)
  Chief Deputy: Anthony Miller
  1230 J Street
  Sacramento 95814
  (916) 445-6371

Controller
Gray Davis (D)
  Chief Deputy: Jim Tucker
  300 Capitol Mall, 18th floor, #100
  Sacramento 95814
  (916) 445-2636

Attorney General
John Van de Kamp (D)
  Chief Deputy: Nelson Kempsky
  1515 K Street, #511
  Sacramento 95814
  (916) 234-5437
  3580 Wilshire Blvd., Room 800
  Los Angeles 90010
  (213) 736-2273

Selected State Departments, Boards and Commissions*

Agricultural Labor Relations Board
  Ben Davidian, Chairman
  915 Capitol Mall, 3rd Floor
  Sacramento 95814
  (916) 322-7007
Air Resources Board
  Jananne Sharpless, Chairwoman
  1102 Q Street
  Sacramento 95814
  (916) 445-4383

Board of Chiropractic Examiners
  Edwward Hoefling, Director
  921 11th St., #601
  Sacramento 95814
  (916) 445-32344
Board of Medical Quality Assurance
  Exec. Dir.: Kenneth J. Wagstaff
  1430 Howe Ave
  Sacramento 95825
  (916) 322-7791
California Coastal Commission
  Peter Douglas, Executive Director
  631 Howard St., 4th Floor
  San Francisco 94105
  (415) 543-8555
California Community Colleges
  John D. Randall, Chancellor (acting)
  1107 9th St., 6th floor
  Sacramento 95814
  (916) 322-4005
California State University
  W. Ann Reynolds, Chancellor
  400 Golden Shore, #324
  Long Beach 90802
  (213) 590-5501
Commission on the Status of Women
  Pat towner, Exec. Direct.
  1303 J St., #400
  Sacramento 95814-2900
  (916) 445-3173
Department of Alcohol and Drug Programs
  Chauncey Veatch, Director
  111 Capitol Mall
  Sacramento 95814
  (916) 455-1943
Department of Consumer Affairs
  Michael Kelley, Director
  1020 N. St., #516
  Sacramento 95814
  (916) 445-4465
Department of Corporations
  Christine Bender, Commissioner
  600 S. Commonwealth Ave.
  Los Angeles 90005
  (213) 736-3481
  1025 P Street
  Sacramento 95814
  (916) 445-8200

*Source: California Department of Finance.

Department of Corrections
Jim Rowland, Director
630 K Street
Sacramento 95814
(916) 445-7688

Dept. of Fair Employment & Housing
Talmadge Jones, Director
1201 I St., #211
Sacramento, CA 95814
(916) 323-5256

Department of Fish and Game
Peter Bontadelli, Acting Director
1416 9th St., #1205
Sacramento 95814
(916) 445-3535

Department of Health Services
Ken Kizer, Director
714 P St., #1253
Sacramento 95814
(916) 445-1248

Dept. of Housing and Community
Develop.
Christine Reed, Director
921 10th St.
Sacramento 95814
(916) 445-4775

Department of Insurance
Roxani Gillespie, Commissioner
100 Van Ness Ave.
San Francisco 94102
(415) 557-3245
Los Angeles 90005
600 S. Commonwealth Ave., 14th Fl.
(213) 736-2551

Department of Mental Health
D. Michael O'Conner, Director
1600 9th St., 1st Floor
Sacramento 95814
(916) 323-8173

Department of Motor Vehicles
A.A. Pierce, Director
2415 1st Ave.
Sacramento 95818
(916) 732-0250

Department of Parks and Recreation
Henry Agonia, Director
1416 9th St., #1405
Sacramento 95814
(916) 445-2358

Department of Transportation
Donald L. Watson, Interim Director
1120 N St.
Sacramento 95814
(916) 445-2201

Department of Veterans Affairs
Jesse Ugalde, Director
1227 O St., #200-A
Sacramento 95826
(916) 445-3111

Department of Water Resources
David Kennedy, Director
1416 9th St., #1115-1
Sacramento 95814
(916) 445-6582

Employment Development
Department
Kaye Rex Kiddoo, Director
800 Capitol Mall
Sacramento 95814
(916) 445-9212

Energy Commission
Charles Imbrecht, Chairman
1416 9th St.
Sacramento 95814
(916) 324-3326

Fair Political Practices Comm.
John H. Larson, Chairman
428 J St., #800
Sacramento 95814
(916) 322-5901

Industrial Welfare Commission
Exec. Officer: Karla M. Yates
525 Golden Gate Ave.
San Francisco 94101
(415) 557-2590

Lottery Commission
Chon Guiterrez, Director
600 N. 10th St.
Sacramento 95814
(916) 324-2025

Native American Heritage Comm.
Larry Myers, Exec. Sec'y
915 Capitol Mall, Room 288
Sacramento 95814
(916) 322-7791

Public Utilities Commission
  Stanley W. Hulett, President
  505 Van Ness
  San Francisco 94102
  (415) 557-3700
State Teacher's Retirement System
  Larry Kurmel, Chief Exec. Officer
  7667 Folson Blvd., 3rd Floor
  Sacramento 95826
  (916) 386-3700
Student Aid Commission
  Samuel Kipp, Exec. Direct.
  1515 S St., #500
  Sacramento 94245-0845
  (916) 445–0880
University of California
  David Gardner, President
  714 University Hall
  Berkeley 94720
  (415) 642-6000
Waste Management Board
  Sherman Roodzant, Chairman
  1020 9th St., 3rd Flr.
  Sacramento 95814
  (916) 322-3330
Wildlife Conservation Board
  W. John Schmidt, Executive Officer
  1416 9th Street, 13th Floor
  Sacramento 95814
  (916) 445-8448
Youth Authority
  Cal Terhun, Director
  4241 Williamsbourgh Dr.
  Sacramento 95823
  (916) 427-6674

California State Senate, 1988*

Alquist, Alfred (D-13)
  AA: Bill Gates
  100 Paseo de San Antonio, #209
  San Jose 95113 (408) 286-8318
  AA: Keith Umemoto
  5100 State Capitol (916) 445-9740

Ayala, Ruben (D-34)
  Dist. Coord.: Wilma Silva
  505 N. Arrowhead Ave., #100
  San Bernardino 92401
  (714) 884-3165
  AA: Michael Valles
  2082 State Capitol (916) 445-6868
Borgeson, Marian (R-37)
  Chief of Staff: Julie Froeberg
  140 Newport Center Dr., #120
  Newport Beach 92660
  (714) 640-1137
  AA: Kevin Sloat
  4082 State Capitol (916) 445-4961
Beverly, Robert (R-29)
  AA: Tom Martin
  1611 S. Pacific Coast Highway
  Redondo Beach 90277
  (213) 540-1611
  AA: Joshua Pane
  2054 State Capitol (916) 445-6447
Boatwright, Dan (D-7)
  AA: Tim Shelley
  1035 Detroit Ave., #200
  Concord 94518 (415) 689-1973
  AA: Barry Brokaw
  3086 State Capitol (916) 445-6083
Campbell, William (R-31)
  AA: Christopher Lancaster
  1661 Hanover Rd., #203
  Industry 91748 (818) 964-1443
  Chief of Staff: Jerry Haleva
  5052 State Capitol (916) 445-2848
Craven, William (R-38)
  AA: Mary Jo Martin
  2121 Palomar Airport Road, #100
  Carlsbad 92009 (619) 438-3814
  Chief of Staff: Scott Johnson
  3070 State Capitol (916) 445-3731
Davis, Ed (R-19)
  Chief of Staff: Hunt Braly
  11145 Tampa Ave., #21B
  Northridge 91326 (818) 368-1171
  Exec. Sec'y: Mavis Friday
  2048 State Capitol (916) 445-8873

*Source: California Department of Finance.

Deddeh, Wadie (D-40)
AA: Barbara Hunsaker
430 Davidson St., Suite C
Chula Vista 92010 (619) 427-7080
AA: Helen Jones
3048 State Capitol (916) 445-6767
Dills, Ralph (D-30)
AA: Rose Sarukian
16921 S. Western Ave., #201
Gardena 90247 (213) 324-4969
AA: Polly Gardener
5050 State Capitol (916) 445-5953
Doolittle, John (R-1)
AA: Mark Thompson
720 Sunrise Ave., #110-D
Roseville 95661 (916) 969-8232
Sr. Consult.: Mark Baughman
5087 State Capitol (916) 445-5788
Ellis, Jim (R-39)
AA: Carol Bentley
2755 Navajo Rd.
El Cajon 92020 (619) 464-7204
AA: Elizabeth Dahl
5082 State Capitol (916) 445-3952
Garamendi, John (D-5)
Dist. Coord.: Larry Sorini
31 East Channel St., Room 440
Stockton 95202 (209) 948-7930
Chief of Staff: John Hendricks
4078 State Capitol (916) 445-2407
Green, Cecil (D-33)
Chief of Staff: Michael McMahan
12631 E. Imperial Hwy. Bg. A, #120
Santa Fe Springs 90670
(714) 670-7196
AA: Rocky Saunders
4081 State Capitol (916) 445-5581
Greene, Bill (D-27)
AA: Walter Backstrom
9300 South Broadway
Los Angeles 90003 (213) 620-5600
AA: Richard Harris
4035 State Capitol (916) 445-2104
Greene, Leroy (D-6)
AA: Fran Burton
P.O. Box 254646
Sacramento 95825 (916) 481-6540
3082 State Capitol (916) 445-7807

Hart, Gary (D-18)
AA: Naomi Schwartz
1216 State St., #507
Santa Barbara 93101
(805) 996-1766
AA: Mimi Modisette
2057 State Capitol (916) 445-5405
Keene, Barry (D-2)
AA: Bunny Lucheta
631 Tennessee St.
Vallejo 94590 (707) 648-4080
Chief of Staff: Charles Cole
313 State Capitol (916) 445-3375
Kopp, Quentin (I-8)
AA: Steve Heminger
363 El Camino Real, #1
S. San Fran. 94080 (415) 952-5666
AA: Dan Friedlander
4062 State Capitol (916) 445-0503
Lockyer, Bill (D-10)
AA: Elsa Ortiz-Cashman
22300 Foothill Blvd., #415
Hayward 94541 (415) 582-8800
AA: Matt Newman
2032 State Capitol (916) 445-6671
Maddy, Ken (R-14)
Field Rep.: Janice DeBenedetto
3443 West Shaw Ave., #100
Fresno 93711 (209) 445-5667
AA: Jo-Ann Slinkard
305 State Capitol (916) 445-9600
Marks, Milton (D-3)
Chief of Staff: Karl Ketner
350 McAllister St., Rm. 2045
San Fran. 94102 (415) 557-1437
AA: Sherill Geiogue
5035 State Capitol (916) 445-1412
McCorquodale, Dan (D-12)
AA: Peggy Collins
100 Paseo de San Antonio
San Jose 95113 (408) 277-1470
Office Coord.: Lee Sturtevant
4032 State Capitol (916) 445-3104
Mello, Henry (D-17)
AA: Kathy Houston
1200 Aguajito Rd.
Monterey 93940 (408) 373-0773
AA: Eva Nelson
5108 State Capitol (916) 445-5843

Montoya, Joseph (D-26)
AA: Michael Duffy
11001 Valley Mall, #204
El Monte 91731 (818) 575-6956
AA: Manuel Zamorano
5064 State Capitol (916) 445-3386
Morgan, Rebecca (R-11)
AA: Nancy Strausser
830 Menlo Ave., #200
Menlo Park 94025 (415) 321-1451
AA: Jon Glidden
4090 State Capitol (916) 445-6747
Nielsen, Jim (R-4)
Dist. Coord.: John Blacklock
1074 East Ave., Suite N
Chico 95926 (916) 343-3546
AA: Jim Kjol
305 State Capitol (916) 445-3353
Petris, Nicholas (D-9)
AA: Audrey Gordon
1111 Jackson St., #7016
Oakland 94607 (415)464-1333
Chief of Staff: Felice Tanenbaum
5080 State Capital
(916) 445-6577
Presley, Robert (D-36)
AA: Tom Mullins
3600 Lime St., #111
Riverside 92501 (714) 782-4111
AA: Carla Anderson
4048 State Capitol (916) 445-9781
Richardson, H.L. (R-25)
AA: Gordon Browning
211 S. Glendora Blvd., Suite C
Glendora 91740 (818) 914-5855
AA: Lorraine Keppel
3063 State Capitol (916) 445-3688
Robbins, Alan (D-20)
AA: Sandy Miller
6150 Van Nuys Blvd., #400
Van Nuys 91401 (818) 901-5555
Assoc. Consultant: Teri Burns
5114 State Capitol (916) 445-3121
Roberti, David (D-23)
Dist. Coord.: Yolanda Gonzalez
3800 Barham Blvd., #218
Hollywood 90068 (213) 876-5200
Chief of Staff: Mel Assagai
205 State Capitol (916) 445-8390

Rogers, Don (R-16)
Field Rep.: Vivian Ferguson
1326 H St., #15
Bakersfield 93301 (805) 395-2927
AA: Beverly Cail
2068 State Capitol (916) 445-6637
Rosenthal, Herschel (D-22)
Chief of Staff: Lynnette Stevens
1950 Sawtelle Blvd., #210
Los Angeles 90025 (213) 479-5588
AA: Colleen Beamish
4070 State Capitol (916) 445-7928
Royce, Edward (R-32)
AA: Marcia Gilcrest
1661 N. Raymond Ave., #211
Anaheim 92801 (714) 871-0270
AA: Joan Bates
4053 State Capitol (916) 445-5831
Russell, Newton (R-21)
AA: Wellington Love
401 North Brand Blvd. #424
Glendale 91203 (818)247-7021
AA: Kay Lentz
5061 State Capitol (916)445-5976
Seymour, John (R-35)
Chief of Staff: Bill Cranham
2150 Towne Center Place, #205
Anaheim 92806 (714) 385-1700
Exec. Admin.: Laurie Hansen
3074 State Capitol (916) 445-4264
Torres, Art (D-24)
Chief of Staff, Bob Morales
107 S. Broadway, #2105
Los Angeles 90012 (213) 620-2529
AA: Elizabeth Bonbright
2080 State Capitol (916) 445-3456
Vuich, Rose Ann (D-15)
AA: Calvin Dooley
120 West Tulare
Dinuba 93618 (209) 591-5005
AA: Marilyn Hawes
5066 State Capitol (916) 445-4641
Watson, Diane (D-28)
Field Rep.: Al Washington
4401 Crenshaw Blvd., #300
Los Angeles 90043 (213) 295-6655
Chief of Staff: Jim Lott
4040 State Capitol (916) 445-5215

California State Assembly, 1988*

Allen, Doris (R-71)
AA: Sam Roth
5911 Cerritos Ave.
Cypress 90630 (714) 821-1500
Legis. Assist.: Donna Burke
4153 State Capitol (916) 445-6233
Arelas, Rusty (D-25)
AA: Carl Guardino
140 Central Ave.
Salinas 93901 (408) 422-4344
Principal Assist.: Kurt Ebans
4139 State Capitol (916) 445-7380
Bader, Charles (R-65)
AA: Diane Stone
203 West G St.
Ontario 91762 (714) 983-6011
AA: Laura Walker
3147 State Capitol (916) 445-8490
Baker, William (R-15)
AA: Jean Meredith
1676 N. California Blvd., #690
Walnut Creek 94596
(415) 932-2537
AA: Ann Jordan
3013 State Capitol (916) 445-8528
Bane, Tom (D-40)
AA: Ann Marcus
5430 Van Nuys Blvd., #206
Van Nuys 91401 (818) 986-8090
Legis. Aide: Lynda Roper
3152 State Capitol (916) 445-3134
Bates, Tom (D-12)
AA: Chapell Hayes
1414 Walnut St.
Berkeley 94709 (415) 540-3176
AA: Amy Strassburg
446 State Capitol (916) 445-7554
Bradley, Bill (R-76)
AA: Virginia Rasmussen
125 W. Mission Ave., #101
Escondido 92025 (619) 489-8924
Exec. Sec'y: Barbara Downs
4177 State Capitol (916) 445-8211

Bronzan, Bruce (D-31)
AA: vacant
2115 Kern St., #205
Fresno 93721 (209) 445-5532
Chief of Staff: Hilary Ross
448 State Capitol (916) 445-8514
Brown, Dennis (R-58)
AA: Greg Hardy
1945 Palo Verde Ave., #203
Long Beach 90815 (213) 493-5514
AA: Bill Bailey
5155 State Capitol (916) 445-8492
Brown, Willie Jr. (D-17)
Chief of Staff: Victoria Lee
350 McAllister, #5046
San Fran. 94102 (415) 557-0784
Chief of Staff: Michael Galizio
219 State Capitol (916) 445-8077
Calderon, Charles (D-59)
AA: Marta Maestas
1712 W. Beverly Blvd., #202
Montebello 90640 (213) 721-2904
AA: Michael Burns
6011 State Capitol (916) 445-0854
Campbell, Robert (D-11)
Chief of Op.: Maria Viramontes
2901 MacDonald Ave.
Richmond 94804 (415) 237-8171
Chief of Staff: Cindy Williams
2163 State Capitol (916) 445-7890
Chacon, Peter (D-79)
Chief of Staff: Irma Munoz
1129 G St.
San Diego 92101 (619) 232-2405
Consult.: Richard Patlan
5119 State Capitol (916) 445-7610
Chandler, Chris (R-3)
AA: Susan Fisk
1227 Bridge St., Suite E
Yuba City 95991 (916) 673-2201
Legis. Assist.: Tracy Sanolin
5136 State Capitol (916) 445-7298
Clute, Steve (D-68)
AA: Steve Burrell
3600 Lime St., #410
Riverside 92501 (714) 782-3222
AA: Dan Boatwright Jr.
4167 State Capitol (916) 445-5416

*Source: California Department of Finance.

Condit, Gary (D-27)
AA: Peggy Crowther
950 10th St., #8
Modesto 95354 (209) 576-6211
Chief of Staff: Mike Lynch
2196 State Capitol
(916) 445-8570
Connelly, Lloyd (D-6)
Field Rep.: Pat McDonald
2705 K St., #6
Sacramento 95816
(916) 443-1183
AA: Tim Howe
2176 State Capitol (916) 445-2484
Cortese, Dominic (D-24)
Principal Assist.: Jim Sparling
100 Paseo de San Antonio, #300
San Jose 95113 (408) 269-6500
AA: Sally Hudson
6031 State Captiol
(916) 445-7558
Costa, Jim (D-30)
AA: Bill Brewster
1111 Fulton Mall, #194
Fresno, 93721 (209) 264-3078
Chief of Staff: Terry Reardon
2111 State Capital (916) 445-7558
Duplissea, William (R-20)
AA: Mike Mahoney
666 Elm St., 2nd floor
San Carlos 94070 (415) 591-5544
Legis. Assist.: Jill Frechette
2130 State Capitol (916) 445-8188
Eastin, Delaine (D-18)
AA: Maureen Hart
39245 Liberty St., Suite D-8
Fremont 94538 (415) 791-2151
AA: Mary Jo Rossi
5175 State Capitol (916) 445-7874
Eaves, Gerald (D-6)
AA: Les Willey
224 N. Riverside Ave., Suite A
Rialto 92376 (714) 820-1902
AA: Debbie Beltram
2188 State Capitol (916) 445-4843
Elder, Dave (D-57)
AA: Janet Keller
245 West Broadway, #300
Long Beach 90802 (213) 590-5009
Chief of Staff: Nathan Manske
4126 State Capitol (916) 445-7454

Farr, Sam (D-28)
Consultant: Laurie Dillon
1200 Aguajito
Monterey 93940 (408) 646-1980 /
Legis. Consult.: Toni Trigueiro
3120 State Capitol (916) 445-8496
Felando, Gerald (R-51)
AA: Lisa Massey
3838 Carson St., #110
Torrance 90503 (213) 540-2123
AA: Elise Mazlum
4162 State Capitol (916) 445-7906
Ferguson, Gil (R-70)
AA: Beverly Evans
4667 MacArthur Blvd., #305
Newport Beach 92660 (714)
756-0665
Chief of Staff: Chris Jones
2016 State Capitol (916) 445-7222
Filante, William (R-9)
AA: Toby Spangler
30 N. San Pedro Rd., #195
San Rafael 94903 (415) 479-4920
Sr. Assist.: John Bovee
5135 State Capitol (916) 445-7827
Floyd, Richard (D-53)
Office Mgr.: Judy Unser
16921 S. Western Ave., #220
Gardena 90247 (213) 516-4037
AA: Georgia King
4016 State Capitol (916) 445-0965
Frazee, Robert (R-74)
AA: Richard Ledford
3088 Pio Pico Drive, #200
Carlsbad 92008 (619) 434-1749
Leg. Sec'y.: Carol MacDonnel
3141 State Capitol (916) 445-2390
Friedman, Terry (D-43)
AA: Elizabeth Cheadle
14144 Ventura Blvd., #100
Sherman Oaks 91423 (818) 501-8991
Sr. Assist.: Elsie Gee
4009 State Capitol (916) 445-4956
Frizzelle, Nolan (R-69)
AA: Jim Orr
17195 Newhope, #201
Fountain Valley 92708
(714) 662-5503
Legis. Assist.: Anita Martin
3098 State Capitol (916) 445-8377

Grisham, Wayne (R-63)
AA: Tony Russo
13710 Studebaker Rd., #202
Norwalk 90650 (213) 929-1796
Legis. Assist.: Lisa Lehman
4017 State Capitol (916) 445-6047
Hannigan, Tom (D-4)
AA: Jim McEnte
844 Union Ave., Suite A
Fairfield 94533 (707) 429-2383
Chief of Staff: Annette Prorini
3104 State Capitol (916) 445-8368
Hansen, Bev (R-8)
Field Rep.: Onita Pellegrini
50 Santa Rosa Ave., #205
Santa Rosa 95404 (707) 546-4500
AA: Joanne Hussey
3151 State Capitol (916) 445-8102
Harris, Elihu (D-13)
AA: Lawrence Reed
1111 Jackson St., #5027
Oakland 94607 (415) 464-0339
Chief of Staff: Valerie Lewis
6005 State Capitol (916) 445-7442
Harvey, Trice (R-33)
AA: Jimmy Yee
2222 E Street, #3
Bakersfield 93301 (805) 324-3300
Legis. Aide: Tracy Williams
4015 State Capitol (916) 445-8498
Hauser, Dan (D-2)
Field Rep.: Sandra Corcoran
1334 Fifth St., Suite G
Eureka 95501 (707) 445-7014
Chief of Staff: Luke Breit
2091 State Capitol (916) 445-8360
Hayden, Tom (D-44)
Sr. Asst.: Carol Kurtz
1337 Santa Monica Mall, #313
Santa Monica 90401 (213) 393-2717
Consultant Christopher Wiley
3091 State Capitol (916) 445-1676
Hill, Frank (R-52)
AA: Kathi Crowley
15111 E. Whittier Blvd., #385
Whittier 90603 (213) 945-7681
AA: Cindy Judy
4130 State Capitol (916) 445-7550

*The 16th Disdtrict is currently vacant
due to the resignation of Democrat
Art Agnos, who was elected mayor
of San Francisco.
Hughes, Teresa (D-47)
AA: Patricia White
3375 S. Hoover St., Suite F
Los Angeles 90007 (213) 747-7451
AA: Joseph Hew Len
3111 State Capitol (916) 445-7498
Isenberg, Phil (D-10)
Dist. Direct.: Holly Liberato
1215 15th St., #102
Sacramento 95814 (916) 324-4676
AA: Alison Harvey
2148 State Capitol (916) 445-1611
Johnson, Ross (R-64)
Dist. Rep.: Phil Miller
1501 N. Harbor Blvd., #201
Fullerton 92635 (714) 738-5853
AA: Linda Brown
4164 State Capitol (916) 445-7448
Johnston, Pat (D-26)
AA: Fran Gottweb
31 E. Channel St., #306
Stockton 95202 (209) 948-7479
Chief of Staff: Jeff Shelton
4112 State Capitol (916) 445-7931
Jones, Bill (R-32)
AA: Michael Chrisman
1441 S. Mooney Blvd., Suite D
Visalia 93277 (209) 734-1182
Legis. Assist.: Vicky Glaser
5160 State Capitol
(916) 445-2931
Katz, Richard (D-39)
AA: James Acezedo
9140 Van Nuys Blvd., #109
Panorama City 91402 (818) 894-3671
Chief of Staff: Kathy Fletcher
3146 State Capitol (916) 445-1616
Kelley, David (R-73)
AA: Margi Weggeland
6840 Indiana Ave., #150
Riverside 92506 (714) 369-6644
AA: Nancy Lucchesi
4158 State Capitol (916) 445-7852

Killea, Lucy (D-78)
  Office Mgr.: Deborah Davis
  2550 5th Ave., #1020
  San Diego 92103 (619) 232-2046
  Principal Consult.: Kathy Krause
  3173 State Capitol (916) 445-7210
Kiehs, Johan (D-14)
  Chief of Staff: Barbara Lloyd
  2450 Washington Ave., #270
  San Leandro 94577 (415) 464-0847
  Principal Consult: Jay Greenwood
  2013 State Capitol (916) 445-8160
LaFollette, Marian (R-38)
  AA: Chris Vosburg
  11145 Tampa Ave., #17A
  Northridge 91326 (818) 368-3838
  Legis. Assist.: Jenifer McDonald
  3132 State Capitol (916) 445-8366
Lancaster, Bill (R-62)
  Field Rep.: Arlo Truax
  145 East Badillo St.
  Covina 91723 (818) 332-6271
  AA: Bill Nunes
  5158 State Capitol (916) 445-9234
Leonard, William (R-61)
  Office Mgr.: Reba Harrison
  1323 W. Colton Ave., #101
  Redlands 92374 (714) 798-4242
  Legis. Assist.: Joan Christensen
  5128 State Capitol (916) 445-7552
Leslie, Tim (R-5)
  Chief of Staff: John Allard
  1098 Melody Lane, #101
  Roseville 95678 (916) 969-3660
  Exec. Sec'y: Jan Prichard
  4116 State Capitol (916) 445-4445
Lewis, John (R-67)
  AA: Allison Rittenhouse
  1940 N. Tustin, #102
  Orange 92665 (714) 998-0980
  Chief of Staff: Margaret Heagney
  5164 State Capitol
  (916) 445-2778
Longshore, Richard (R-72)
  AA: Scott Taylor
  14550 Magnolia St., #201
  Westminster 92683 (714) 895-4334
  Legis. Aide: Earlene Arnold
  5126 State Capitol (916) 445-7333

Margolin, Burt (D-45)
  AA: Bunny Wasser
  8425 West 3rd St., #406
  Los Angeles 90048 (213) 655-9750
  Legis. Assist.: Karen Yamamoto
  4117 State Capitol (916) 445-7440
McClintock, Tom (R-36)
  Chief of Staff: M. Means-Lauffer
  350 N. Lantana, #222
  Camarillo 93010 (805) 987-9797
  Legis. Assist.: Tracy Morgan
  4102 State Capitol (916) 445-7402
Mojonnier, Sunny (R-75)
  AA: Christopher Heiserman
  3368 Governor Drive, Suite C
  San Diego 92122 (619) 457-5775
  AA: Shirley Schleber
  4005 State Capitol (916) 445-2112
Moore, Gwen (D-49)
  AA: Joy Atkinson
  3731 Stocker St., #106
  Los Angeles 90008 (213) 292-0605
  Admin. Aide: Amy King
  2117 State Capitol (916) 445-8800
Mountjoy, Richard (R-42)
  AA: Peggy Mew
  201 N. 1st Ave.
  Arcadia 91006 (818) 446-3134
  AA: Cecilia Ward
  2175 State Capitol (916) 445-7234
Nolan, Patrick (R-41)
  Sr. Assist.: Bob Haueter
  143 S. Glendale Ave., #208
  Glendale 91205 (818) 240-6330
  Chief of Staff: Richard Temple
  2114 State Capitol (916) 445-8364
O'Connell, Jack (D-35)
  AA: Carla Fisk
  Studio 127 El Paseo
  Santa Barbara 93101
  (805) 966-2296
  AA: Cara Johnson
  2141 State Capitol (916) 445-8292
Peace, Steve (D-80)
  AA: Carmen Sandoval-Fernandez
  430 Davidson St., Suite B
  Chula Vista 92010 (619) 426-1617
  Chief of Staff: David Takashima
  4140 State Capitol (916) 445-7556

Polanco, Richard (D-55)
  Chief of Staff: Sandra Chacon
  110 North Ave., #56
  Los Angeles 90042
  (213) 255-7111
  Legis. Aide: Chris Flammer
  2170 State Capitol (916) 445-7587
Quackenbush, Charles (R-22)
  Sr. Assist.: Janice Ploeger
  456 El Paseo de Saratoga
  San Jose 95130 (408) 446-4114
  Legis. Sec'y: Kim Weideman
  5150 State Capitol (916) 445-8305
Roos, Michael (D-46)
  Sr. Assist.: Mary Chambers
  625 S. New Hampshire Ave.
  Los Angeles 90005 (213) 386-8042
  Chief of Staff: Rich Milner
  3160 State Capitol (916) 445-7644
Roybal-Allard, Lucille (D-54)
  AA: Martha Molina
  5261 E. Beverly Blvd.
  Los Angeles 90022 (213) 721-5557
  AA: Maria L. Ochoa
  5140 State Capitol (916) 445-1670
Seastrand, Eric (R-29)
  AA: Leslie Ramsey
  523 Higuera St.
  San Luis Obispo 93401
  (805) 549-3381
  Leg. Assist.: Mary Ann Coppinger
  4144 State Capitol (916) 445-7795
Sher, Byron (D-21)
  AA: Betsy Shotwell
  785-C Castro St.
  Mountain View 94041
  (415) 961-6031
  Chief Consult.: Kip Lipper
  2136 State Capitol (916) 445-7632
Speier, Jackie (D-19)
  Field Rep.: Pat Lloyd
  510 Myrtle Ave., #107
  S. San Fran. 94080 (415) 871-4100
  AA: Michael Thompson
  5156 State Capitol (916) 445-8020
Statham, Stan (R-1)
  Field Rep.: Marilyn McCarthy
  429 Red Cliff Drive, #200
  Redding 96002 (916) 223-6300
  AA: Patrick Murphy
  4098 State Capitol (916) 445-7266

Stirling, Larry (R-77)
  AA: Walter Slater
  7777 Alvarado Rd., #377
  La Mesa 92041 (619) 237-7777
  Exec. Sec'y: Barbara Reynolds
  2137 State Capitol (916) 445-6161
Tanner, Sally (D-60)
  Exec. Sec'y: Rita Snykers
  11100 Valley Blvd., #106
  El Monte 91731 (818) 442-9900
  Exec. Sec'y: Cathy Craft-Foreman
  4146 State Capitol (916) 445-7783
Tucker, Curtis (D-50)
  AA: Patricia Decuir
  1 Manchester Blvd.
  Inglewood 90306 (213) 412-6400
  AA: Tracey St. Julien
  2158 State Capitol (916) 445-7533
Vasconcellos, John (D-23)
  AA: Scott Strickland
  100 Paseo de San Antonio, #106
  San Jose 95113 (408) 288-7515
  Sr. Consult.: Michael Twombly
  6026 State Capitol (916) 445-4253
Waters, Maxine (D-48)
  Field Rep.: Mike Davis
  7900 South Central Ave.
  Los Angeles 90001 (213) 582-7371
  Chief of Staff: Simpson Fontaine
  5016 State Capitol (916) 445-2363
Waters, Norman (D-7)
  AA: Joe Ryan
  250 Main St.
  Placerville 95667 (916) 626-4954
  Sr. Consultant: Ron Lawton
  6028 State Capitol (916) 445-8343
Wright, Cathie (R-37)
  Field Rep.: Michael Murphy
  250 East Easy St., #7
  Simi Valley 93065 (805) 522-2920
  AA: Catherine Morrison
  3126 State Capitol (916) 445-7676
Wyman, Phil (R-34)
  AA: Diane Oglesby
  5393 Truxtun Ave.
  Bakersfield 93309 (805) 395-2673
  Legis. Aide: J. David Alexander
  2170 State Capitol (916) 445-3266
Zeltner, Paul (R-54)
  AA: Guy Weeks
  16600 Civic Center Dr., #233
  Bellflower 90706 (213) 920-9755
  Legis. Assist.: Carrie Harper
  5130 State Capitol (916) 445-7486

Directory of Political Organizations . . .

American Civil Liberties Union (civil liberties defense)
633 S. Shatto Place
Los Angeles, CA 90005

Asian Pacific Legal Center (civil rights issues)
1010 S. Flower
Los Angeles, CA 90015

Building Industry Association (pro-growth)
1571 Beverly Blvd.
Los Angeles, CA 90026

California Labor Federation, AFL-CIO (labor)
995 Market Street, Suite 310
San Francisco, CA 94103

California Public Interest Research Group (CALPIRG) (consumer
and environmental issues)
1147 S. Robertson Blvd. Suite 203
Los Angeles, CA 90035

Campaign California (economic justice and environmental issues)
1337 Santa Monica Blvd., Suite 301
Santa Monica, CA 90401

Central American Refugee Center (CARECEN) (refugee resettlement)
660 S. Bonnie Brae
Los Angeles, CA 90057

Chamber of Commerce of the United States (business association)
1615 H Street NW
Washington, DC 20062

Coalition for Clean Air (air quality issues)
309 Santa Monica Blvd., Suite 212
Santa Monica, CA 90401

Common Cause (quality of government issues)
2030 M Street NW
Washington, DC 20036

Democratic State Central Committee (partisan)
6380 Wilshire Blvd., Suite 1615
Los Angeles, CA 90048 (213) 655-2494

Friends Committee on Legislation (religious nonpartisan)
926 J Street, Room 707
Sacramento, CA 95814

Japanese American Citizens League (civil rights)
1765 Sutter Street
San Francisco, CA 94115

Libertarian Party (third party)
301 W. 21st
Houston, TX 77008

Mexican American Legal Defense and Education Foundation
(civil rights)
634 S. Spring Street, 11th floor
Los Angeles, CA 90014

National Association for the Advancement of Colored People
(civil rights)
4805 Mt. Hope Drive
Baltimore, MD 21215

National Gay and Lesbian Task Force (civil rights)
1517 U Street NW
Washington, DC 20009

National Organization for Women (women's issues)
1410 New York Avenue NW
Washington, DC 20005

Peace and Freedom Party (third party)
P. O. Box 54397
Los Angeles, CA 90054

Planning and Conservation League (environmental issues)
909 12th
Sacramento, CA 95814

Republican State Central Committee (partisan)
1228 N Street, Suite 14
Sacramento, CA 95814 (916) 443-0967

Save-the-Redwoods League (conservation issues)
114 Sansome Street, Rm. 605
San Francisco, CA 94104

Sierra Club (environmental issues)
730 Polk Street
San Francisco, CA 94109

Toward Utility Rate Normalization (TURN) (consumer issues)
2550 Ninth Street, Suite 1038
Berkeley, CA 94710

Voter Revolt (to cut insurance rates)
407 State Street
Santa Barbara, CA 93102

Index

California
  and citizens, 2–3
  Constitutional development, 11–15
  and the nation, 3–4
California Association of Realtors, 22, 88
California Bar Association, 59
California Club of Los Angeles, 16
California courts, 55–60
California Democratic Council (CDC), 30
California executive, 46–54
California Journal, 27
California Labor Federation, 22
California legislature, 41–45
California Medical Association, 22
Californians, 5–10
California politics
  national impact, 1–2
  period divisions, 12–13
  in perspective, 1–4
  and political parties, 26–32
California Republican Assembly (CRA), 30
California State Assembly, members, 106–10
California State Senate, members, 103–6
California Supreme Court, 13, 16, 17, 57
California Teachers Association, 22
Californocracy, 2
Cal-OSHA, 3, 47
Campaign for Economic Democracy, 31
Campaign reform, 35–36
Campaigns, and elections, 33–40
Catholic Church, 11
CDC. *See* California Democratic Council (CDC)
Center for Continuing Study of the California Economy, 32
Charter city, 68
Chen, Lily, 20

Chinese exclusion provisions, 18
Chinese immigrants, 13
Christian Scientists, 17
Citizens, of California, 2–3
City governments, 67–73
  creating, 67–68
  and finances, 72–73
  forms of, 68–71
  and politics, 71–72
Civil law, and criminal justice, 61–66
Civil liberties, 16
  defined, 95
Civil rights, 16
  defined, 95
Civil service system, 27
  defined, 95
Clay, Henry, 12, 95
Clemency, defined, 96
Closed primary, 33
  defined, 95
Columbus, Christopher, 11
Commissions, state, 101–3
Committees, and California legislature, 44–45
Common Cause, 32, 35
Compromise of 1850 (Clay), 12, 95–96
Conference committee, 44–45
  defined, 96
Constitution, California
  amendment procedures, 14
  basic principles, 15
  current, 13
  development, 11–15
  and freedom of religion, 16–17
  unitary system, 15
Constitutional officers, 100–101
  defined, 96
Constitutional offices, 52
Constitutional Revision Commission, 13
Consumer Revolt Initiative, 25
Consumer Services Agency, 102
Consumers' Union, 25